FEATURE EXTRACTION APPROACHES FOR OPTICAL CHARACTER RECOGNITION

FEATURE EXTRACTION APPROACHES FOR OPTICAL CHARACTER RECOGNITION

ROMAN V. YAMPOLSKIY

Rochester Institute of Technology

Briviba Scientific Press

Rochester, NY

FEATURE EXTRACTION APPROACHES FOR OPTICAL CHARACTER RECOGNITION

COPYRIGHT (c) 2007 Roman V. Yampolskiy, Briviba Scientific Press

ISBN: 978-0-6151-5511-1

To My Parents

Contents

List of Figures

10

Preface

Since the 1950's character recognition has been an active field of research for computer scientists worldwide. The main reason is that character recognition is not only an interesting area of theoretical research with relevance to many pattern recognition sub-fields, but also a very needed and useful real-life application. Making computers able to read would allow for substantial savings in terms of the costs for data entry, mail processing, form processing and many other similar situations. Additionally, this can simplify the life of the handicapped by making computers able to read out loud to visually impaired.

Every realistic character recognition system requires a feature extraction step in order to properly operate. This book begins with large-scale review of the feature extraction approaches for character recognition based on both literature review and experimental results. Both universal (designed for large number of different data sets) and specific (aimed at a particular type of characters) methods are included in this review.

An original classification system was developed, which groups feature extraction methods depending on their theoretical approach. The developed classification system aids in comparison and analysis of the feature extraction methods. Classification has been verified by the character recognition experiments, which confirmed its validity. Representative subset of all the feature extraction methods reviewed has been selected for more detailed analysis and implementation. The subset included at least a few methods from each cluster generated by the developed classification system.

Next, analysis, optimization and comparison of two different classifiers, namely Multiple Layer Perceptron Network and Radial Basis Function Network were conducted. Optimal parameters for learning rate, spread, momentum, number of layers, number of nodes and number of epochs for this particular application were found. Radial Basis Function Network was chosen as the superior classifier, both in terms of its speed and accuracy.

A novel feature extraction method, called Fuzzy Zoning, was developed. Fuzzy Zoning's main competition was with other zoning approaches and unlike all of them, it was designed to counteract the problem of sharp zone borders by allowing a single pixel to contribute to multiple zones at the same time. Fuzzy Zoning was analyzed and included in the classification with other zoning based features.

Based on experiments and test results, all feature extraction methods were ordered against their accuracy. As this ordering didn't consider time complexity required of the classifier to work with a particular feature, the size of the feature vectors was taken into consideration for comparison purposes.

A new metric was developed, which was called Normalized Accuracy Measure. Unlike a simple accuracy, this metric considers time complexity of feature classification. This approach allows optimizing the total character recognition operation, which includes both feature extraction and classification. All feature extraction methods were compared and ordered against the developed Normalized Accuracy Measure metric.

Keywords: *Feature Extraction, Optical Character Recognition, Normalized Accuracy Measure, Fuzzy Zoning, Invariance, Handwritten, Classifier, Off-line features, Pattern Recognition, Neural Network, Radial Basis Function Network, Multiple Layer Perceptron Network, Handprinted, Projection Histogram, N-tuple, Hough Transform, Chain Code Transform, Gabor Filter, Feature Points, Strokes, Character Profiles, Graph Description, Characteristic Loci, Shadow Code, Template Matching, Zoning, Angular Partitions, Radial Coding, Concentric Circles, Tracks and Sectors, Ring Projection, Crossing Method, Moments, Geometric, Central, Transformed, Gegenbauer, Legendre, Tchebichef, Krawtchouk, Zernike, Pseudo-Zernike, Fourier-Mellon, Wavelets, Fractal Encoding, Fractal Feature, Structural, Statistical, Feature Taxonomy, Classification*

23

Chapter 1

Introduction

> *The beginning of knowledge is the discovery of something we do not understand.*

Frank Herbert (1920 - 1986)

1.1   Introduction to Character Recognition

Since the 1950's Optical Character Recognition, or OCR, has been an active field of research for computer scientists worldwide [185]. The main reason is that OCR is not only an interesting area of theoretical research with relevance to many pattern recognition sub-fields, but also a very needed and useful real-life application.

Making computers able to read paper documents would allow for substantial savings in terms of the costs for data entry, mail processing, tax form processing, census form processing and many other similar situations. Additionally, this can simplify the life of the handicapped by making computers able to read out loud to visually impaired.

Modern OCR systems are able to recognize most printed fonts and even some neat handwritten text with acceptable accuracy. As a result, the current research in OCR has shifted towards omnifont machine printed text, and unconstrained handwritten text as well as towards increase in the overall recognition accuracy [185].

1.2   Pattern Recognition System

All complete OCR systems consist of multiple processing steps, namely: image acquisition, preprocessing, feature extraction, classification, and finally, postprocessing. In this work, we will concentrate on the feature extraction step, since selection of good features is arguable the most important step towards achieving high levels of accuracy by the OCR system.

1.2.1   Data Collection

Data collection approaches can be as diverse as the character data itself, from optical scanners to onscreen pointers. Regardless of the type of devise producing the image of the pattern, data is usually collected in a very raw state. Typical sources of data include postal zip codes and addresses, census form data, surveys, medical reports, etc. The handwritten text is typically comprised of whole words not isolated characters and one of the first steps is to break up sentences into words and words into individual symbols. The resulting images of individual symbols are what we need as input data for the character recognition system.

1.2.2   Preprocessing

Preprocessing involves cleaning up the data and trying to make it as easy to classify as possible. The cleaning of data includes filling of gaps and removal of noise, both byproducts of image acquisition process or of the later character segmentation algorithm. Examples of a gap and noise are demonstrated in the Figure 1.1. Usually a filter is used on the image to close the gaps and to remove noise particles, which are typically detected based on their small size with respect to the main pattern.

Additional preprocessing may be needed in case of color or grayscale images. Normally color images are rare and are easily converted to grayscale. Grayscale images need to be binarized for which a thresholding algorithm is utilized, with the finding of the optimal threshold value being the most challenging part of the process. The result is an image comprised of just two values typically 0 and 1, which serve as the input to the feature extraction algorithm.

Another step, called *normalization*, may be present if we desire to obtain an image, which is processed to counteract the effects of *translation*, *scaling*, and *rotation*. In each of those special situations a particular algorithm can be applied:

Translation This is the case in which the pattern is located off the center of the image containing the pattern. To fix this the pattern could be shifted, for example, to the point where its upper-left corner lines up with a particular pixel in the image.

Rotation This is the case in which the pattern is oriented in a way, which is different from the one in which human reader would typically read it. This could range from just a few degree of difference to a complete upside-down pattern. There is no easy to apply solution as knowing by how much to rotate the pattern requires first to recognize it, and this of course is not possible at this step.

Scaling This is the case in which the pattern is stretched or truncated and so it is hard to recognize due to the difference in size. This is easy to fix by rescaling the pattern to some standard size expected of all patterns being processed.

Figure 1.1: A gap and noise in the character 'I' [119].

1.2.3   Feature Extraction

Since direct processing of scanned characters images is computationally pro-
hibitive, the widely accepted technique of pattern recognition is to extract
some features from the original data and perform classification on those features. Extracted features must have certain properties in order to achieve
low error rates in character classification. Features must provide maximum
amount of information about the original pattern, ideally completely describing it. The total number of features should be minimized to reduce burden
on the classification step. This means that used features should be independent of each other in order to maximize entirety of provided information [119].

Since the same character can look very different if it is translated, scaled,
rotated, stretched, or skewed, ideally we are interested in finding features,
which remain constant under the above-mentioned morphing. If features
with such properties cannot be extracted, an alternative is to use image normalization with respect to the size, rotation, and thickness of the character.
Unfortunately, this method has a down side of introducing new errors into
the data. Not the least of the good properties of a pattern's feature is a high
tolerance to the noise and degradation in the original image, as well as the
complexity of the computation of the feature [185, 119].

An important characteristic of a good pattern's feature is reconstructability,
which means that the feature contains enough information to reconstruct the
original pattern. While not always achievable, reconstructability is a desirable property because it serves as a proof that the feature contains all the
needed information to recognize the pattern in question. For some features,
such as infinite series coefficients only partial reconstruction of the original
image is possible since only a small subset of an infinite series is used as a
feature. The idea is that if such small subset is sufficient to reconstruct the
original pattern even approximately, the features must have high information
content and so poses high discrimination power [185].

1.2.4   Classification

Classifier is one of the most important parts of any pattern recognition system. The job of the classifier is to look at the feature vector extracted from
the pattern and determine to which class does this particular character be-

longs. A large number of different classifiers exist, but they all can be grouped under the following headings:

Template Matching Each pattern is compared against all other already classified patterns and the set to which the closest match belongs is selected as the probable class of the pattern.

Statistical Classifiers In this approach a function is designed, which has the property of subdividing the feature space with hyperplanes so characters of different types a separated into different regions.

Artificial Neural Networks Based on the neural networks found in nature, those interconnected tiny computing devices come together to prove that sometimes the whole is greater than the sum of its parts. This is the approach often tried in different fields of artificial intelligence and particularly in computer vision and pattern recognition. Detailed introduction to the theoretical properties of Artificial Neural Networks could be found in Chapter 3.

Decision Trees Determine type of the pattern based on the set of rules; each designed to further subdivide patterns until the identity of the pattern becomes obvious.

1.2.5   Postprocessing

This is an optional step, which typically involves correction of errors and reconstruction of the original document. Once each individual symbol has been recognized, the symbols are grouped together to form words. Then words are compared against a dictionary to see if such combinations of characters exist in the language.

A simple spellchecker could be used to replace an unexisting word with the correct one. Additionally, the words surrounding the one in question could be used to improve the corrective ability of the spellchecker. Such systems are particularly good at working with postal addresses since the domain is very limited and well established. Once the error correction is complete the entire document could be reconstructed in the textual format as apposed to the image format.

Chapter 2

Feature Extraction Methods

There is much pleasure to be gained from useless knowledge.

Bertrand Russell (1872 - 1970)

2.1   Features Utilized by a Human Reader

In construction of the program capable of 'reading' individual characters, it may be valuable to consider how the best-known system for the purpose - a human being operates. What features do human readers utilize during character recognition process, and could we teach the machines to use the same ones? Those are the questions answers, to which may come as extremely beneficial to construction of a high accuracy pattern recognition system.

It is a well-known fact that people rarely have to recognize individual characters in isolation. The typical task of reading consists of recognizing symbols, which make up complete words. As established by many experiments, the meaning of a word, as well as the shape of the word contribute to the correct recognition of individual characters. This is something not typically programmed into the character recognition software, at least not prior to a few years ago [192].

In research into reading, as in most of psychology, observing the type of errors made under hard circumstances is a very fruitful type of investigation. Bouma [192] investigated the features unconsciously extracted by human

29

subjects during the task of character recognition. He presented character symbols to the subjects at a distance or for a very short duration of time, and examined the confusions made between different letters. Bouma grouped the characters of the English alphabet into sets based on the errors made by the subjects in his experiments. The Bouma's classification of *psychologically close* letters is presented in Figure 2.1.

Outer contour	Bouma shape	Code	Letters
Short	inner parts and rectangular envelope	1	a s z x
	round envelope	2	e o c
	oblique outer parts	3	r v w
	vertical outer parts	4	n m u
Tall	ascending extensions	5	d h k b
	slenderness	6	t i l f
Projecting	descender	7	g j p q y

Figure 2.1: Bouma's classification of letters [192].

The classification consists of three large sets, namely Short, Tall and Projecting characters, which are further subdivided into as many as four subgroups with up to five characters in each.

The actual features believed to be used by human readers vary by a researcher. Hubel and Wiesel believe the features are generated early in the visual cortex. The complex cells they found detect the presence of bars and edges and provide a representation of lines. McGraw et al. conducted experiments with machine printed characters and found that high-level structural descriptors of letters are very likely utilized. For example, a letter 'b' could be described as a loop with a stroke attached at the lower right. Intuitively, this latter representation seems very close to a human heart, but we can not dismiss the value of unconscious processes [192].

Later in the chapter we will see that both types of features are indeed put to work in the task of machine character recognition by various researchers.

2.2   Image Partitioning Approaches

2.2.1   Zoning, a.k.a. Sub-window Pixel Count

The method of zoning was introduced in 1972 by Hussain, [75]. It is one of the easiest feature extraction methods in terms of implementation. The feature produced is an array of integers representing the number of turned-on pixels in the sub-windows of an original image. Refer to figure 2.2 for a visual representation of the above idea.

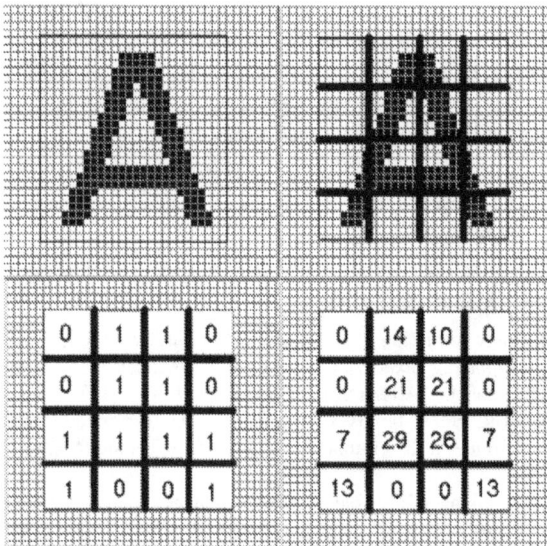

Figure 2.2: Upper-left: character A; Upper-Right: Zoning grid imposed; Lower-Left: binary zoning feature; Lower-Right: sub-window pixel counts

In more formal terms the idea is to sub-divide the bilevel image into K non-overlapping regions or zones R_i, $i = 1...K$, each of size $h \times v$. In this case the feature f_i is the number of foreground pixels in R_i. This results in a K dimensional feature vector [119].

The number of sub-windows, K, used during feature extraction, can vary from as little as one, giving us the area of the binary image, to the total number of pixels in the image, $h \cdot v$, resulting in image itself. Smaller sub-window size results in better discriminatory performance, since in large sub-windows important pattern information gets smashed. Typically, a window size of 4×4 or 8×8 is used. The resulting feature vector remains relatively small, even as a size of the input image increases. For example, even in a small 30×30 pixel image using 5×5 sub-windows we end up with a 36-dimensional vector.

In the original paper Hussain *et al.* [75], summarized the desirable properties of their proposed feature extraction algorithm as follows:

- The feature vector is obtained from the pattern matrix by a repetitive procedure involving only the simple logical operation of counting the number of black points in a well-defined region.

- The feature vector's dimensionality is significantly lower than that of many other schemes and the features themselves assume only a relatively small number of values.

- Discontinuities in the character matrix, including salt and pepper noise, can be tolerated [75].

An additional reduction in the complexity of an extracted feature can be achieved by replacing pixel counts for each sub-window with a binary flag signifying state of the pattern in this region. See bottom-left of figure 2.2 for an example of so called binary-zoning feature. Unfortunately this strategy significantly reduces a discriminatory ability of the zoning feature.

In addition to being applicable to binary images, zoning can be used on gray scale images as well. In order to extract the feature vector, an average gray level is computed as can be seen in figure 2.3. Unfortunately, the resulting feature is not illumination invariant [185].

Zoning method is a universal feature extractor, capable of operating on binary, gray scale, contour, and even skeleton character representations. But, it does have some obvious problems, such as its lack of tolerance for either rotation, shifting or scaling. While invariance is a desirable property of a good feature, through some clever preprocessing we can almost completely overcome this obvious shortcoming.

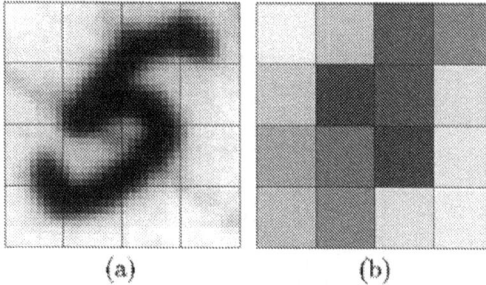

Figure 2.3: Zoning on a gray level image. (a) A 4 × 4 grid on a gray scale character. (b) The resulting average gray levels for each zone [185].

Zoning Pseudonyms

It is a well-known fact, that sometimes in the process of scientific discovery different researches stumble upon the same idea independently of one another. Nothing is truer about feature extraction methods, in particular *Zoning*. While it is most popular under that name, it is not at all uncommon to read about it under a pseudonym.

For example in this book it is referred to as pixel-sub count method. It is described as *Density Feature* in the work of Bajaj et al. [7] named after a small modification, namely normalization process in which the sum of the pixels in each subwindow is being divided by the total number of pixels in that zone, resulting in the black pixel density for that region. The same feature without modifications is called *Averaging Algorithm* in the paper by Torok et al. [184]. Finally Hanmandlu et al. [62] refers to it as *Box Approach*. Such multitude of names makes comparison of works by different researchers more complicated and hopefully this book will be a step towards universal naming convention for different features used in character recognition.

2.2.2   Fuzzy Zoning

The method of *Fuzzy Zoning* (FZ) developed by the author is aimed at introducing a certain degree of tolerance for small changes in character's shape, position and size, which cause problems for the classical zoning approach.

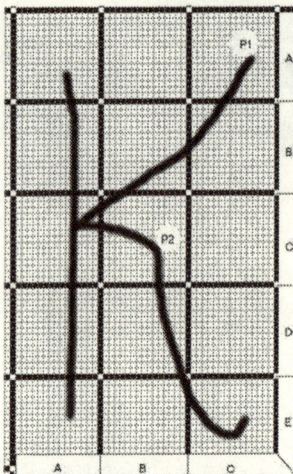

Figure 2.4: Fuzzy contribution of pixels located in a corner or in a middle of a pattern.

The main problem with the zoning method is its reliance on rigid zone borders. Each pixel either contributes to a particular zone or does not, depending on its location. This has particularly negative effect in case of near-border pixels as even the smallest shift in the pattern results in a different feature vector. Cao at el. attempted to counteract this problem by creating something called *Fuzzy Borders* (FB). The main distinction of FB lays in the fact that points of the pattern located near zone borders are given fuzzy membership values in up to four zones at the same time. Fuzzy membership values are normalized by always adding up to one for all zones [23].

Taking the idea behind FB and expanding on it we came up with the concept of FZ. Unlike in a case of FB in which only border-pixels have fuzzy properties and only in up to four different zones, our method gives all pixels fuzzy membership values and ability to contribute in up to nine neighboring zones at the same time. The contribution of each individual pixel in the original image depends on its relative location within the zone as well as within the global pattern. Figure 2.4 demonstrates this idea. Pixel $P1$ located in zone CA contributes heavily to that zone since it is located almost in a middle of it, but it also contributes, but to a much lesser extent, to zones CB, BB and BA. Pixel $P2$ located in zone BC also contributes heavily to its home zone, but it also contributes, to zones AD, AC, AB, BB, CB, CC, CD and BD.

The actual contribution of each pixel to each zone depends on the distance between the pixel and the zone and is automatically calculated by performing multiplication operation between the original pattern and the special fuzzy-mask developed by us. The fuzzy-mask is a group of concentric squares whose weighted value diminishes linearly as the distance from the center of the mask increases. Figure 2.5 is a sample fuzzy-mask with linear decrease in pixel contribution of 10 percent for each concentric square. By moving the fuzzy-mask across the entire original pattern, we were able to obtain FZ feature vector consisting of 25 individual elements each representing a unique zone and the fuzzy contribution of the zone's neighbors.

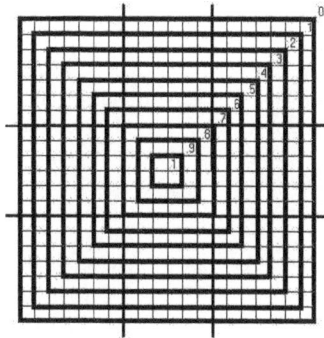

Figure 2.5: Fuzzy mask with linear decrease in pixel contribution of 10 percent for each concentric square.

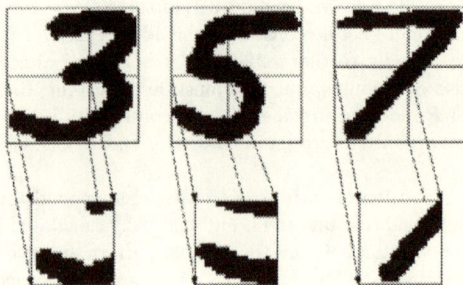

Figure 2.6: Discriminative ability of local information [136].

2.2.3 Zoning - Meta Feature

Zoning feature has already been described in section 2.2.1, where it was equated with the sub-window pixel counts. In that case, the image was subdivided into zones and for each zone an area of the character pattern falling in that zone was computed. The concept of zoning can be abstracted into the so-called meta-feature, by saying that it simply involves breaking the original image into a number of subzones. The resulting subzones can be processed with any feature extraction method described in this book. The resulting feature vectors can be concatenated into one comprehensive feature vector describing the overall pattern.

The main advantage of the zoning meta-method is that the properties of individual subparts of the image are not mixed, but extracted separately. This allows for local information to play a more significant role in pattern classification. It is a well-known fact that local information is often all you need to distinguish patterns belonging to a particular subset of all possible patterns. Figure 2.6 demonstrates how digits '3' and '5' can be ruled out if local information in just one subzone is more typical of a digit '7's pattern [136].

Unfortunately, the nature of zoning method itself leads to a very serious shortcoming, namely artificially set-up zone borders introduce increased de-

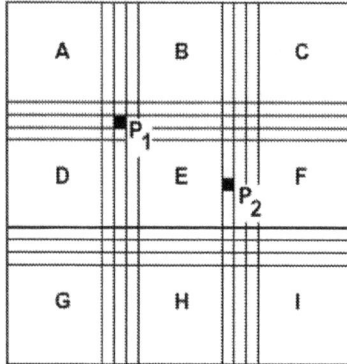

Figure 2.7: Zoning method with fuzzy borders. Pixel P_1 has a fuzzy membership value of .25 in each of the four zones A, B, D, and E. P_2 has a .75 membership value in zone E and .25 in zone F [185].

gree of variation into the feature subvectors. The subpatterns may show up differently in subwindows due to even small shape variations in the whole pattern, resulting in radical differences in the values computed for subvectors, which in turn makes the concatenated final feature vector less continuous pattern descriptor [94]. Cao at el. attempted to counteract this problem by creating something they called *fuzzy borders*. The main distinction of fuzzy borders is in the fact that points of the pattern located near zone borders are given fuzzy membership values in up to four zones at the same time. Fuzzy membership values are normalized by always adding up to one for all zones [23]. Figure 2.7 demonstrates zoning with fuzzy borders.

Since the zoning method as presented here is just a way to break up the original image, we are still faced with a choice of feature extraction method to be used with our subdivision approach. Different researchers have tried out different feature extraction methods with varying degrees of success. Examples of some of the features utilized are described below. In general, practically any feature extraction method described in this book can be used in conjunction with subzoning technique.

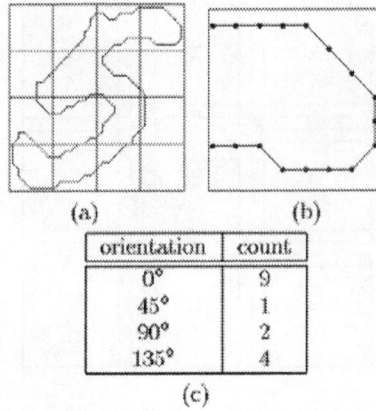

orientation	count
0°	9
45°	1
90°	2
135°	4

(c)

Figure 2.8: Zoning combined with contour line segment counts. (a) character subdivided into 16 equally sized zones; (b) contour lines in the upper-right zone only; (c) count of contour lines for this zone. [185].

Kimura and Shridhar worked with contour curves as the pattern representation technique. After applying zoning they grouped the contour line segments based on orientation into four subgroups, namely: horizontal, vertical, diagonal (45° and 135°) orientations. The number of contour segments belonging to each group was used as the extracted feature for each zone. Figure 2.8 demonstrates this approach [89]. Another researcher, Takahashi, also used orientation histograms, but in addition he also found high curvature points along the contour. For each such point, Takahashi computed contour tangent, curvature value, and position within the zone [185].

Singh and Hewitt [160] used a modified Hough transform (see Section 2.6.3 for details) in combination with nine 3×3 windows in their work on cursive digit and character recognition.

Hanmandlu et al. [62], developed a feature they call the *box approach*, which is undoubtedly based on zoning. After the pattern is projected onto the zoning grid, a particular point is taken to be the absolute origin $(0,0)$.

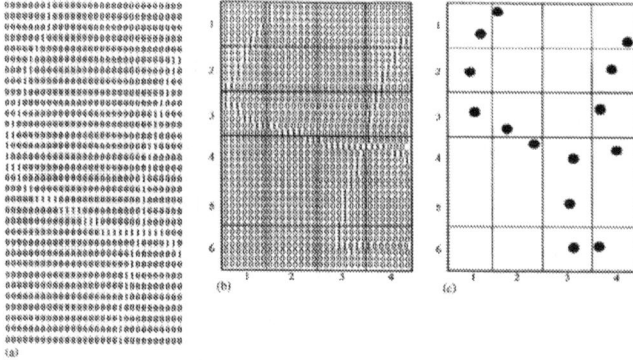

Figure 2.9: (a) Normalized digit 4. (b) Digit 4 partitioned into 6 × 4 boxes. (c) pattern of digit 4 plotted using extracted features [62].

For example in [62] bottom left corner of the original image is used for such purpose. The vector distance for kth pixel in bth box at location (i, j) is calculated as, $d_k^b = (i^2 + j^2)^{\cdot}5$. By dividing the sum of distances of all set-on pixels present in the box by their total number, a normalized vector distance for each box is computed as follows:

$$\gamma_b = (1/n_b) \sum_{k=1}^{n_b} d_k^b, b = 1, ..., 24 \qquad (2.1)$$

where n_b is the number of pixels in the bth box. The resulting vector comprises a set of features based on distance. For each set-on kth pixel in a box, the corresponding angle is computed as, $\theta_k = \arctan(-j/i)$ for a pixel at (i, j). Then the sum of all angles in a box b is normalized with the number of set-on pixels present in that box to get a normalized angle α_b.

$$\alpha_b = (1/n_b) \sum_{k=1}^{n_b} \theta_k^b, b = 1, ..., 24 \qquad (2.2)$$

The resulting 24 pairs comprise the complete feature set used by [62] for recognition. Figure 2.9 (c) demonstrates the points extracted from digit '4', using zoning based box approach feature.

An interesting modification to the concept of zoning is dynamic zoning, which is not based on a set number of equal-in-size zones, but rather the number and size of zones and their positioning depends on the pattern itself. Lecce at al. [96] proposed a technique for automatic zoning, which is based on Shannon's entropy estimation. *Core* zones of pattern are determined, which provide the highest discriminatory ability, and the final zoning is being custom fitted around such core locations within the image.

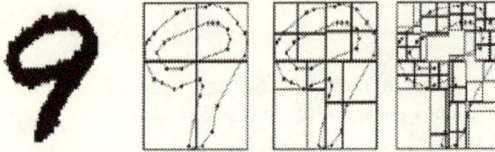

Figure 2.10: Zoning using a quad tree [181].

In a similar fashion, Teredesai at al. [181] developed a quad tree based zoning method. An example of their technique can be seen in figure 2.10. The first subfigure shows the original input pattern. The second figure shows that pattern divided into four zones. The remaining figures demonstrate further zoning of the pattern, based on the amount of details desired to be obtained from each local location within the image [181]. Since, certain locations are particularly useful in segregation of similar patters, this type of zoning is designed to allow the character recognition system to zoom in on points of interest in the pattern and as a result, distinguish particularly challenging data inputs. The strength of this approach is in its customization with respect to the problem at hand. The method takes advantage of all available information about possible classification types for our particular input and is closely related to the properties of the pattern we are trying to recognize.

2.2.4 Angular Partitions

Proposed by Tsang Ing Ren, et al. [147, 146] as recently as 1998, angular partitions represent another way of subdividing an original pattern into subparts. The number of partitions can be varied from as few as one, in which case the whole image is subject to the further processing, to partitioning the image completely by lines. Clearly both of those extreme cases are not a useful application of angular partitioning. An intermediate number of partitions were shown by Tsang et al. to lead to acceptable levels of recognition. They have also concluded that the optimal number of partitions exists and it is problem depended. In order to achieve some degree of invariance, the center of mass of the pattern is used as the origin point for the partitioning rays.

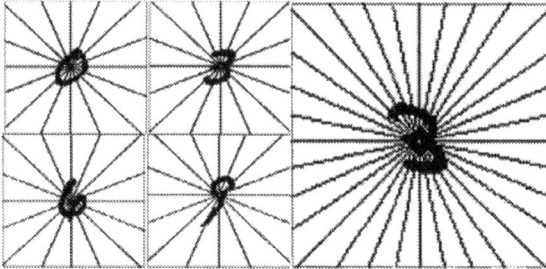

Figure 2.11: Left: Digits '0', '3', '6', and '9' with 16 angular partitions. Right: Digit '3' with 32 Angular partitions [147, 146].

Once the original image is subdivided, an additional feature extraction method needs to be applied to each subzone. In their work, Tsang et al. used Radial moments in order to derive the necessary pattern description. See Section 2.4.4 for additional information about Radial moments.

Figure 2.11 demonstrates four sample digits subdivided into 16 angular partitions as well as the digit '3' with 32 angular partitions. A small problem with this methodology can be observed, namely the implementation. Since the input pattern for character recognition is not continuous, but made up of binary pixels, it is not straightforward to subdivide the image into angular partitions as it is, for example, with simple zoning (see Section 2.2.1). Tsang, et al., suggest using Bresenham's line algorithm, which is an efficient way for scan-converting straight lines. Any line drawing algorithm can in principal be used as long as the resulting partitioning is equivalent.

As with the zoning meta-feature (see Section 2.2.3), angular partitioning is not a feature extraction method; it is actually a way of subdividing the original image into smaller segments on which the actual feature extraction will be done.

2.2.5 Radial Coding a.k.a. Concentric Circles

While investigating the application of moments of inertia (see Section 2.4.1 for details) to character recognition problems Torres-Mendez, et al. [183] observed that some characters had the same or very close moment-of-inertia value produced, which made accurate classification extraordinary difficult. In order to combat the above-described problem, they decided to introduce additional features into the character recognition process. Named *Radial Coding*, it was designed with intention of achieving rotation invariance in order to complement translation and scale invariant capability of moment of inertia used as the primary feature [183].

Figure 2.12: Differences between the letters 'M' and 'N' [183].

The circle shape was chosen as the natural rotation invariant base for the Radial Coding. The number of intensity pixel changes on a circular boundary of some radius inside the object is used in this simple coding method. A compilation of such measurements from multiple concentric circles forms the feature vector, which is invariant to translation, scaling and rotation. Unfortunately, the possibility of multiple characters mapping onto the same extracted feature was not eliminated with the introduction of Radial Coding. This is demonstrated in Figures 2.12, 2.13, 2.14 and 2.15 with respect to characters 'M' and 'N'.

In the second attempt to circumvent insufficient uniqueness of resulting features, Torres-Mendez, et al. [183], proposed an additional step in which they take into consideration the difference between the size of the two largest

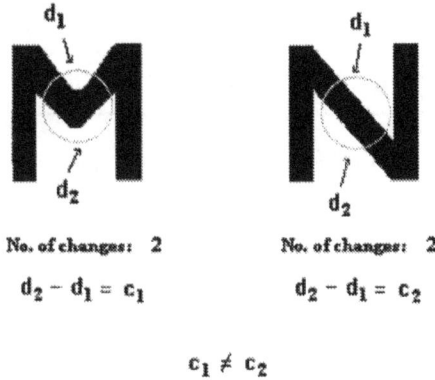

Figure 2.13: Difference in size of the two largest arcs outside the pattern for the letters 'M' and 'N' [183].

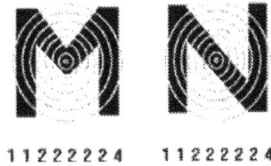

Figure 2.14: Concentric circles applied to letters 'M' and 'N' [183].

arcs (for each concentric circle) that not belong to the pattern. Those are demonstrated in Figures 2.13. Dividing this difference by the circumference of the respective concentric circle results in size normalization. The algorithm for extracting Radial Coding as presented in [183] is:

1. Find the central moment of the object.

2. Compute K equidistant concentric circles C_i around the centroid located in step 1. The spacing is equal to the distance between the centroid and the furthest pixel of the pattern divided by the total number of concentric circles.

Circle Letter	2	3	4	5	6	7	8
N	0	0.08	0.08	0	0.03	0.02	0.01
M	0	0.18	0.41	0.26	0.18	0.06	0.01

Figure 2.15: Normalized differences obtained for the letters 'M' and 'N' [183].

3. For each concentric circle, count the number of intensity changes (zero to one or one to zero) that take place in the pattern. Call this value R_i.

4. For each concentric circle, calculate two largest arcs that are not part of the pattern. Determine each arc by counting the number of arc pixels, obtain the difference, and divide by the circumference. This is $D_i = (d_1 - d_2)/d_c$ where d_1 is the length of the largest arc, d_2 is the length of the second largest arc, and d_c is the circumference [183].

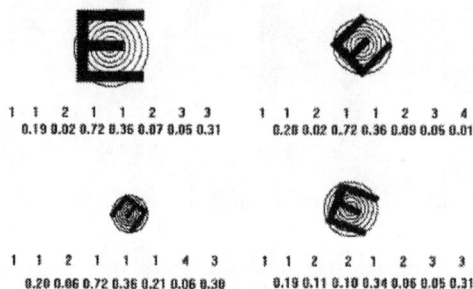

1 1 2 1 1 2 3 3
0.19 0.02 0.72 0.36 0.07 0.05 0.31

1 1 2 1 1 2 3 4
0.20 0.02 0.72 0.36 0.09 0.05 0.01

1 1 2 1 1 1 4 3
0.20 0.06 0.72 0.36 0.21 0.06 0.30

1 1 2 2 1 2 3 3
0.19 0.11 0.10 0.34 0.06 0.05 0.31

Figure 2.16: Concentric circles applied to letter 'E', shown in different rotations and sizes. Numbers in the first line indicate the number of intensity pixel changes in each one of the eight circumferences. Second line represents the normalized differences over the largest seven circumferences [183].

The above algorithm gives us the feature vector: $R_1, R_2, ..., R_K, D_1, D_2, D_K$ assuming K concentric circles. R_i is a positive integer, and D_i is a real value in the range $[0, 1]$. Both the Radial Coding and Normalized Radial Coding

features have the property of being invariant to rotation, scaling, and translation. Taken combined with moments of inertia, those features allow sufficient
uniqueness of final feature vectors to achieve problem free classification of 2D
patterns, in particular alphanumeric characters. Figure 2.16 shows feature
vectors extracted from the character 'E' under different rotation and scale
values. The top line is the number of intensity pixel changes and the bottom line is the normalized difference over the largest seven concentric circles
[183].

2.2.6   Tracks and Sectors

Sometimes, a new feature is just a clever combination of some older sim-
pler features. This is just the case with the method of *Tracks and Sectors*.
Clearly inheriting and combining structural properties from methods of *Angular Partitions* and *Concentric Circles* and Ring Projections (see Sections
2.2.4, 2.2.5, 2.3.2 for details) this feature is a close relative of meta-feature
known as zoning (see Section 2.2.3).

Tracks-and-Sectors zoning image subdivision method is aimed at taking
advantage of circular nature of many handwritten symbols. The methodology can be applied to either binary or gray scale images. Just like with
Angular Partitions approach, we begin by finding the centroid of the image,
utilizing the zero and first order moments for this purpose. Next, the image
is subdivided into n sectors formed by drawing n radical lines from the centroid at an angle θ to each of other such that $n\theta = 360^\circ$ [38].

As with the Concentric Circle and Ring Projection methods, m concentric
circles are drawn with the centroid of the pattern as center such that each
band or *ring* between any two consecutive circles has the same area. This
requirement is achieved by computing the radius r_j of the jth circle by the
following formula:

$$r_j = \sqrt{\frac{j}{m}} r_m \qquad (2.3)$$

where r_m is the distance between centroid and the farthest point of the
image from it. As a result, the pattern is divided into $n \times m$ segments [38].
Figure 2.17 demonstrates this for $n = 12$ sectors and $m = 3$ tracks. Figures
2.18 and 2.19 shows application of the Tracks and Sectors method to some

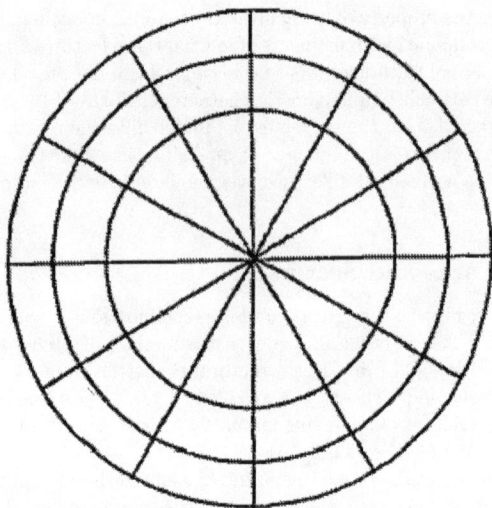

Figure 2.17: A segmentation scheme with 12 sectors and 3 tracks [38].

alphanumeric symbols.

Just like with the meta-feature Zoning, different second order feature extraction methods can be used in conjunction with the Tracks in Sectors method. Ashwin et al. [5] take a classical approach and use the set-on pixel count for each zone as their feature used in recognition of Kannada characters. Belongie et al. [10] refer to this method as *log-polar histogram bins* and combine it with shape contexts in a technique reminiscent of deformable template matching. Hong [69] and Desai et al. [38] suggest using Radial moments (see Section 2.4.4 for addition information) to achieve an interesting and highly discriminative feature extraction scheme.

The method of Tracks and Sectors can be made invariant to translation, rotation and scale changes of the pattern by including a few additional post-

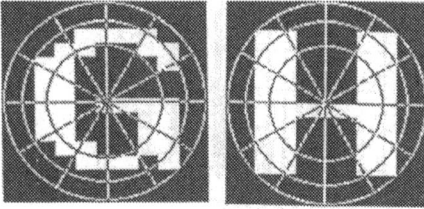

Figure 2.18: Semented images of characters 'G' and 'H' [38].

Figure 2.19: Segmented image of digit 6 [69].

processing steps. First, let us assume that the feature vector, regardless of secondary feature extraction method, is represented by:

$$X = [x_1, x_2, ..., x_{nm}]$$

In order to realize translation invariance, we need to move the origin to the centroid of the pattern. This is easily done by transforming the image $f(x, y)$ into $f(x + x_0, y + y_0)$, where (x_0, y_0) is the centroid of the pattern [38].

Scale invariance results from normalization of the feature vector. X is transformed to X^s by

$$X^s = \frac{X}{x^{max}} \tag{2.4}$$

where $X^{max} = max(X)$.

Finally, rotation invariance is achieved by some clever shifting within the feature vectors corresponding to individual bands. Each feature subvector is shifted until the maximum value feature becomes the first element of the subvector, and relative order of the features remains the same for that subvector. Obviously, X^R is independent of the orientation of the pattern. To demonstrate the above idea more formally, a mathematically expressed example follows [38]. Given a feature vector X in the form:

$$X = [[x_1, x_2, ..., x_{M_1-1}, x_{M_1}, x_{M_1+1}, x_{1 \times n}]$$

47

$$[x_{n+1}, x_{n+2}, ..., x_{M_2-1}, x_{M_2}, x_{M_2+1}, x_{2\times n}]$$

$$...$$

$$[x_m, x_{m+1}, ..., x_{M_m-1}, x_{M_m}, x_{M_m+1}, x_{m\times n}]]$$

$$X_{M_i} \geq x_j$$

$$(i-1) \times n < j < r \times n$$

$$1 \leq i \leq m$$

each subvector represents the feature values corresponding to a particular track. If more than one maximum value happens to be in a particular band, the second largest value is selected instead. X is transformed to X^R so

$$X^R = [[x_{M_1}, x_{M_1+1}, ..., x_{1\times n}, x_1, x_2, x_{M_1-1}]$$

$$[x_{M_2}, x_{M_2+1}, ..., x_{2\times n}, x_{n+1}, x_{n+2}, x_{M_2-1}]$$

$$...$$

$$[x_{M_m}, x_{M_m+1}, ..., x_{m\times n}, x_m, x_{m+1}, x_{M_m-1}]]$$

Finding the maximum value for each subvector instead of a global maximum, allows us to reduce the chance of getting different segments with maximum values for different orientations, scales and noises. The fact, that secondary feature for each track-sector region can be computed completely independently of other such regions allows for parallel implementation of this particular feature, resulting in extremely fast processing [38].

2.3 Histogram Based Approaches

2.3.1 Projection Histograms

Introduced by Glauberman in 1956, this is one of the oldest known feature extraction methods. In addition to being utilized as a feature for character recognition it is also an effective and popular method for text preprocessing used for word or character segmentation as well as determination of the orientation of scanned text.

Traditionally as a character's feature, only the horizontal and vertical pattern histograms were extracted, as can be seen in figure 2.20. In such a case, a feature represents a projection of the original pattern onto the x and y axes. For the horizontal projection, the total number of turned on pixels for each column x_i is calculated and saved. The same procedure is done for the vertical projection with respect to columns y_j, where i varies from 1 to W and j varies from 1 to H.

An alternative way of thinking about his feature is to understand that we are aiming at reducing 2D characters to a 1D signal in order to simplify the work of our classification module. We can think of a slit that scans the character from left to right. By projecting the shadow cast by character from the light coming out of the slit onto the x-axis, we are in effect transforming a two-dimensional geometric shape into a one-dimensional light distribution shed on the axes. Additional processing can be applied to the 1D signal in order to make it more useful to the classification task. Sections on Wavelets and Fourier series expansion will provide the detailed description of possible alternatives. Figure 2.21 (a) shows numeral 4 being scanned by a slit of light, while part (b) of the same figure demonstrates the resulting one-dimensional projection [127].

This feature can be made scale-independent if a fixed number of bins are used instead of taking image dimension in pixels as the number of bins. Simply merging neighboring bins into groups and dividing by the total number of set pixels in the image would satisfy this requirement. This feature is also extremely sensitive to rotation and slightest differences in character representation, which results in problems with recognition of different writing styles in case of hand written characters. Additionally, while the vertical

Figure 2.20: Horizontal and vertical projection histograms for digit five [185].

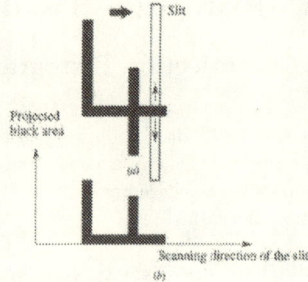

Figure 2.21: 2D reduction to 1D using a slit of light [127].

projection histogram is slant invariant, its horizontal counterpart is not [185].

In order to measure the dissimilarity between two projection histograms we can use:

$$dissimilarity = \sum_{i=1}^{n} \mid y_1(x_i) - y_2(x_i) \mid \tag{2.5}$$

where n is the number of bins, and $y1$ and $y2$ are the two histograms we wish to compare. Unfortunately, this dissimilarity measure is sensitive to slight misalignment of dominant peaks in the original projection histograms. We can reduce the effects of this problem by using *cumulative histograms* $Y(x_k)$, defining the sum of the first k bins to be:

$$Y(x_k) = \sum_{i=1}^{k} y(x_i) \tag{2.6}$$

we can rewrite equation 2.22 to be:

$$Dissimilarity = \sum_{i=1}^{n} \mid Y_1(x_i) - Y_2(x_i) \mid \tag{2.7}$$

where Y_1 and Y_2 are the two cumulative histograms.

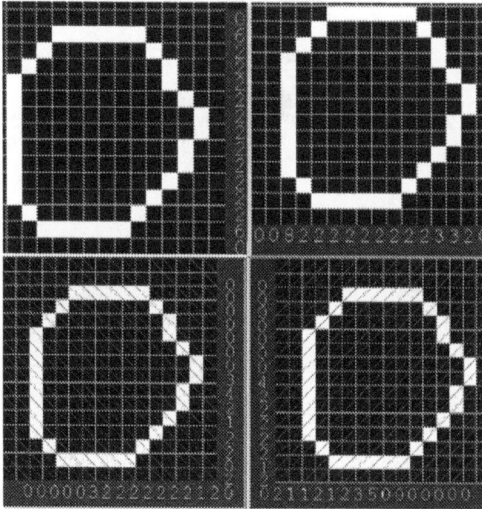

Figure 2.22: Horizontal, Vertical, Left diagonal, and Right diagonal projection histograms [163].

In addition to horizontal and vertical histogram projections, it is possible to extract both left and right diagonal projection histograms. Just like their more popular horizontal and vertical cousins, they have a straightforward definition, namely they are defined as the count of the number of set pixels per diagonal. Combination of all four projection histograms is used by [163] in his character recognition project. Figure 2.22 demonstrates computation of all four projection histograms, for a sample handwritten character zero. Combing all for projection histograms we get:

[0 0 6 2 2 2 2 2 2 2 2 2 2 2 6 0] +
[0 0 8 2 2 2 2 2 2 2 2 2 3 3 2 0] +
[0 0 0 0 0 0 0 4 2 2 2 2 2 1 2 0 2 1 1 2 1 2 3 5 0 0 0 0 0 0 0] +
[0 0 0 0 0 3 2 2 2 2 2 2 2 1 2 0 2 0 2 2 1 2 4 3 0 0 0 0 0 0 0]

a 94-feature vector, which [163] uses as input to a neural network classifier.

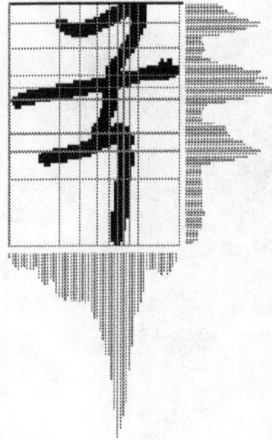

Figure 2.23: Horizontal and vertical projection histograms on a mesh partitioned Korean character [93].

Figure 2.24: Horizontal and vertical projection histograms of Marathi character [145].

In all cases, additional information or sub-features can be extracted from projection histograms, Ravindra [145] proposes extracting actual character's height, width and area as well as maximum values for all projections. That information can be used instead of actual projection-histogram-information in order to reduce computational complexity. An example of vertical and horizontal projection histograms can be seen in the Figure 2.24.

The problems with the projection method became painfully obvious after examining figure 2.25, which shows how two different geometric shapes can produce perfectly identical projection histograms [127].

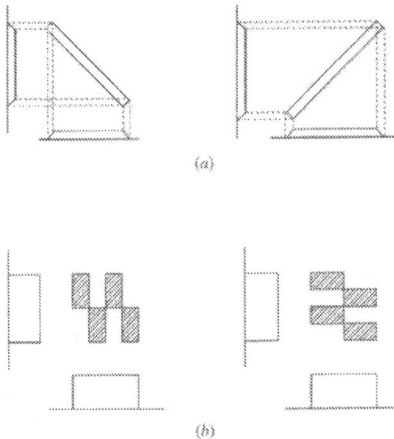

(a)

(b)

Figure 2.25: Different geometric shapes can produce identical projection histograms [127].

Due to their poor performance on even slightly rotated images, projection histograms are rarely used as a stand-alone character feature, rather they are combined with other features to provide additional useful information [94]. For example Soo [93] supplements his Directional Segment Feature with a projection histogram in order to improve recognition of Korean handwritten characters. Figure 2.23 demonstrates the extracted vertical and horizontal projection histograms for a Korean character partitioned with a 9×9 mesh.

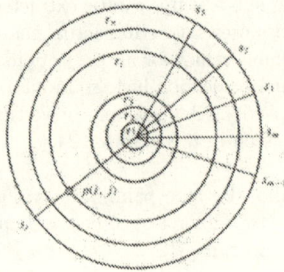

Figure 2.26: Ring Ex-
traction panel [173].

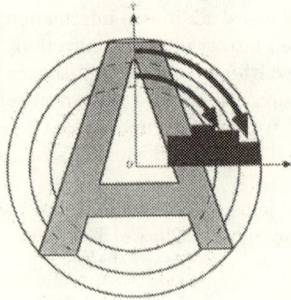

Figure 2.27: Ring pro-
jection [173].

2.3.2   Ring Projections

Projection Histograms described in Section 2.3.1 have one major shortcoming, namely complete inability to deal with rotations of even small degree
in the pattern. In order to combat this problem, a ring-based projection
method was conceived. This method takes advantage of rotation invariant
properties of the circular shapes of any radius.

Ring Projection, a method that is described in great detail in Tang [173]
and in Phokharatkul [143]. This method utilizes a ring-extraction panel
which is defined as a triple $\Phi = (R, \Theta, \delta)$, where $R, \Theta \in I$, and δ, the ring-
extraction function, is a function of R and Θ, meaning $\delta = p(R, \Theta)$, and

$$\forall_{k \in I}[p(R, \Theta) = p(R, \Theta + km)] \qquad (2.8)$$

where $p(R, \Theta)$ is a cycle function of Θ with a period of m. A visual representation of the ring-extraction panel is given in Figure 2.26. It consists of
n concentric circles and m spokes, where n and m are both integers. The
radius of the ith ring (R_i) is denoted by r_i, and s_i represents the jth spoke
($i = 1, 2, ..., n; j = 1, 2, ..., m$). Each cross point between a ring and a spoke
is called a *sample point*, $p(i, j)$ represents the cross point between the ith
ring and the jth spoke [173]. After being processed by the Ring Extraction
panel, a pattern is converted into a vector called a *Ring Projection vector*,

which is defined as:

$$\vec{V} = [p_{r_1}, p_{r_2}, ..., p_{r_n}] \tag{2.9}$$

$$\vec{V} = \left[\int_1^m p(1,j)dj, \int_1^m p(2,j)dj, ..., \int_1^m p(n,j)dj \right] \tag{2.10}$$

Since we are dealing with the discrete digital image the ring-projection vector is:

$$\vec{V} = \left[\sum_{j=1}^m p(1,j)dj, \sum_{j=1}^m p(2,j)dj, ..., \sum_{j=1}^m p(n,j)dj \right] \tag{2.11}$$

and

$$p(i,j) = \begin{cases} 1, overlaps\ with\ the\ given\ pattern \\ 0, otherwise \end{cases}$$

The basic principle of the Ring Projection feature extraction methodology can be seen in Figure 2.27. The pixels of the pattern are projected along the rings, and not along the straight lines as in the Projection Histogram approach. This results in the fundamental difference between the two methodologies, namely rotation invariants [173].

Transformation Ring Projection

1. Locate the center of gravity and translate it to the origin of the image.

2. Find the largest distance d.

3. Scale the input image by D/d.

4. Find the ring-projection vector using the ring-projection operation.

5. Find the feature vector by accumulating the p_{r_i}'s.

Position invariance is easily achieved by moving the center of gravity of the pattern to the origin $(0,0)$. Detailed description of this idea can be found in Section on Geometric Moments 2.4.1. Size invariants is obtained by finding the pixel farthest away from the center of pattern, let's call it d. Normalization of the size results from dividing pattern size - D by d found previously. Rotation invariance comes directly from fundamental properties of Ring Projection approach [173].

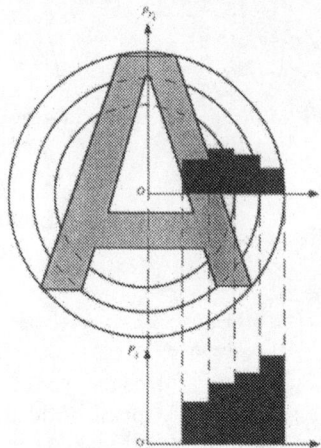

Figure 2.28: Ring Projection associated with accumulation [173].

Finally, while the ring-projection values p_{r_i}'s may be acceptable for classification, they would be changed if the center of gravity is shifted due to the noise in the image or as the result of round-off error caused by the discrete nature of the digital images. In order to counteract that, an accumulation operation shown in Figure 2.28 is utilized. Accumulation operation produces the feature vector consisting of P_i elements as shown below:

$$[P_1 \ P_2 \ P_3 ... P_n]^T$$

where each element P_i is defined as in below:

$$P_i = \sum_{k=1}^{i} p_{r_k} \sum_{k=1}^{i} \sum_{\theta=0}^{2\pi} f * (k, \theta), \quad i = 1, 2, ..., n \qquad (2.12)$$

This approach of using accumulated projections, to substitute the individual projections of a ring is more stable according to Tang et al. [173].

2.4 Method of Moments

In general, moments describe numeric quantities at some distance from a reference point or axes [21]. Moments achieved status of some of the most popular image descriptors, used in visual pattern recognition, shortly after Hu introduced them in 1961. Since that time, moments have been used for aircraft identification, building and bridge identification, scene analysis, target classification, and OCR. Many variations on the basis concept exist, including fast algorithms and three-dimensional moments [119].

The $(p + q)$th order moment, where $p, q \geq 0$, of a function $f(x, y)$ is defined in terms of double integral as:

$$m_{pq} = \int_{-\infty}^{+\infty} \int_{-\infty}^{+\infty} x^p y^q f(x, y) dx dy$$

If $f(x, y)$ is piecewise continuous and has non-zero values in the region of interest, then the moments of all orders exist and the *uniqueness* theorem can be proved:

Uniqueness Theorem: The sequence $\{m_{pq}\}$, $p, q \geq 0$, is unequally determined by $f(x, y)$, and conversely, $f(x, y)$ is unequally determined by $\{m_{pq}\}$.

The above theorem insures that an image may be assigned a unique set of moments, and as a result be properly classified [119].

Over a dozen of different moment based feature extraction approaches have been proposed specifically targeting character recognition problem. The following sections will cover some of the most promising and well-documented methodologies.

In general for all moment methods, the feature vector can be build by taking n first moments and combining them, as bellow:

$$[m_0, m_{01}, m_{10}, ..., m_{pq}], \; where \; n = p + q$$

Most moment based approaches extract statistical features, which have no clear meaning to a human observer. This is particularly true for higher order moments. This makes it difficult to properly evaluate quality of the extracted moment based feature. One workaround for this problem is the idea of image reconstruction. Basically, given n moments of a particular type, researcher tries to reconstruct the original image from those n moments. The results are judged by a human observer, who visually evaluates how much of the original pattern is reconstructed, and decides if it is possible for him to recognize the pattern in question.

An insightful reader will note that good reconstructive ability of the feature does not always translate into good interclass discrimination ability and vise versa. This is certainly true, but high reconstructability property, means that a large percentage of original pattern is preserved in the feature and so the feature provides all the needed information to allow for successful character discrimination.

Some of the following subsections, which describe particular moment based feature extraction methods are accompanied by pictures showing reconstructed sample character images up to some moment n. They are included solely to allow the reader of this book to visually evaluate information-preserving properties of particular moments. Image reconstruction or compression is beyond the subject of this book.

2.4.1 Geometric Moments

Known under such names as *Regular*, *Geometric*, *Classic* or *Conventional* two-dimensional moments are presented below.

In case of a discrete digital image, the summations are used in place of the integrals in the definition of the m_{pq} moment. Given an image f, of size $W \times H$ the conventional raw moments may be computed by [119]:

$$m_{pq} = \sum_{x=0}^{W-1} \sum_{y=0}^{H-1} x^p y^q f(x, y)$$

The complete *moment set* $\{m_{pq}\}$ of order n is composed of moments m_{pq}, $p + q \leq n$. This set contains $\frac{1}{2}(n + 1)(n + 2)$ elements [112].

The moments presented below can be used to compute simple mechanical and statistical values that may be used as features.

0th Order Moment: Mass

The 0th moment:

$$m_{00} = \sum_{x=0}^{W-1} \sum_{y=0}^{H-1} f(x,y)$$

represents the mass of the given distribution function or image $f(x,y)$ based on its intensity. In terms of binary images zeroth order moment is just the total area of the represented object [21, 119].

1st Order Moments: Center of Mass

In physics, center of mass refers to actual, physical mass of the body. In digital images we are dealing with individual pixels. So, in terms of a binary function, in which the only possible resulting values are 0 or 1, the center of mass or first order moment is simply the average x and y position, based on set pixels, in the object representation. Two different 1st order moments can be found:

$$m_{10} = \sum_{x=0}^{W-1} \sum_{y=0}^{H-1} x f(x,y)$$

$$m_{01} = \sum_{x=0}^{W-1} \sum_{y=0}^{H-1} y f(x,y)$$

This center of mass point is know as centroid or Ω (also known as *center of gravity, average* or *arithmetic mean*. The coordinates $\bar{x}$ and $\bar{y}$ of Ω are defined by:

$$\bar{x} = \frac{m_{10}}{m_{00}} \quad and \quad \bar{y} = \frac{m_{01}}{m_{00}}$$

If Ω is used as the new point of origin in the image, the moments extracted from such image are known as *Central moments*, and can be computed as follows [21, 119]:

$$\mu_{pq} = \sum \sum (x - \bar{x})^p (y - \bar{y})^q f(x,y) dx dy$$

2nd Order Moments: Average energy

The second order moments:

$$m_{11} = \sum_{x=0}^{W-1} \sum_{y=0}^{H-1} xy f(x,y)$$

$$m_{20} = \sum_{x=0}^{W-1} \sum_{y=0}^{H-1} x^2 f(x,y)$$

$$m_{02} = \sum_{x=0}^{W-1} \sum_{y=0}^{H-1} y^2 f(x,y)$$

are called the moments of inertia [1] [111]. They may be used to define several useful mechanical object features such as: *mean square value* or *average energy* [21]. Second order moments can also be used to determine the principal axes of the shape [111].

If we are working with Central moments, we can define an image ellipse which is an elliptical disk, centered at Ω, and which has the same second order moments as the original pattern. The ellipse is defined by:

$$a = \left(\frac{2\left[\mu_{20} + \mu_{02} + \sqrt{(\mu_{20} - \mu_{02})^2 + 4\mu_{11}^2}\right]}{\mu_{00}} \right)^{\frac{1}{2}}$$

$$b = \left(\frac{2\left[\mu_{20} + \mu_{02} - \sqrt{(\mu_{20} - \mu_{02})^2 + 4\mu_{11}^2}\right]}{\mu_{00}} \right)^{\frac{1}{2}}$$

and its axes coincide with the axes of the original image.

---

[1] An interesting anecdote is associated with the discovery of application of moments-of-inertia to character recognition problem. A graduate student named Sigfried in the 1970's was interested in doing research in character recognition for his master's thesis. He was aware of a variety of techniques described in literature for extracting descriptors of shape, but he wanted to come up with his own approach. Sigfried had just finished reading a book on lateral thinking by Edward de Bono. One of the ideas behind lateral thinking is to use randomness to arrive at new ideas and Sigfried decided to use this method to find his own feature extraction method. Sigfried decided to browse through the books in the library by flips of the coin. With his first flip he ended up in the engineering library. Another flip directed him to civil engineering section. A further flip of the coin led him to open a book on dynamics. After flipping through a few pages, he hit upon images of what looked to him like characters. In reality it was a chapter on Moments of Intertia of common geometric objects. Sigfried quickly realized that he had stumbled upon a novel feature extraction approach, he rushed back to his office to tell his roommate he had found a topic for his thesis [187].

Orientation of the ellipse and so the orientation of the original pattern can be found by:

$$\phi = \frac{1}{2}\tan^{-1}\frac{2\mu_{11}}{\mu_{20} - \mu_{02}}$$

where ϕ is the angle between x-axis and the nearest axis of the ellipse [119].

3rd Order Moments: Skewness

The third order Central moments define the *skewness* S_x and S_y of the image projections. This is a measure of the deviation from the symmetry about the mean of the distribution. The S_x and S_y have the following definitions [119]:

$$S_x = \mu_{30}/\mu_{20}^{\frac{3}{2}} \quad and \quad S_y = \mu_{03}/\mu_{02}^{\frac{3}{2}}$$

4th Order Moments: Kurtosis

The fourth order Central moments define the *kurtosis* of the pattern. Kurtosis is the degree of how peaked the statistical distribution of data is relative to a normal distribution. The Kurtosis is defined as a normalized form of the fourth central moment of a distribution and is found as follows:

$$K_x = \mu_{40}/\mu_{20}^2 - 3 \quad and \quad K_y = \mu_{04}/\mu_{02}^2 - 3$$

Higher Order Moments

As the degree of the moment gets larger, the statistical or mechanical meaning of it tends to become more obscure; nevertheless, as many as 500 moments have been used in pattern recognition and in image reconstruction [119, 193].

2.4.2 Normalized Central Moments

Central moments are first introduced in the Section 2.4.1 on Geometric moments as they are closely related to each other. Just to recap, if center of mass is used as the new origin point in the image, the moments extracted from such image are known as *Central moments*, and can be computed as follows [21, 119]:

$$\mu_{pq} = \sum\sum(x - \bar{x})^p(y - \bar{y})^q f(x,y)dxdy$$

Normalized Central Moments are defined as:

$$\eta_{pq} = \frac{\mu_{pq}}{\mu_{00}^{\gamma}}$$

where

$$\gamma = \frac{p+q}{2} + 1$$

In 1962 Alt defined another representation of Normalized Central Moments, which possess desirable invariant properties. The proposed formulation is presented bellow [94]:

$$m_{pq}^{*} = \frac{\sum_{x=1}^{w} \sum_{y=1}^{h} x^{*p} y^{*q} f(x,y)}{m_{00}}$$

where

$$x^{*} = (x - \frac{m_{10}}{m_{00}})/\sqrt{\mu_{20}/m_{00}}, \quad and \quad y^{*} = (y - \frac{m_{01}}{m_{00}})/\sqrt{\mu_{02}/m_{00}}$$

2.4.3 Moments of Transformed Patterns

One of the greatest challenges of character recognition is the variability presented in the encountered examples. In most cases, position, size and orientation of the test symbols is not the same as in the training cases. It led researchers to investigate behavior of moments extracted from the transformed image f'. Moments presented bellow are derived for translated, scaled, rotated or reflected images [119]:

Translation: The translation of the pattern f by a vector $\vec{V}(V_x, V_y)$ results in an image $f\prime$, such that: $f\prime(x,y) = f(x-V_x, y-V_y)$. The translated moment is given by [22, 119]:

$$m_{pq}' = \sum \sum (x - V_x)^p (y - V_y)^q f(x,y)$$

It is clear that if the moments are computed with respect to the centroid of the image, they are invariant to translation.

Scaling: The scaling of the image f by factors α and β in x and y directions, results in $f'(x, y) = f(x/\alpha, y/\beta)$. The scaled moment is given by [22, 119]:

$$m'_{pq} = \int \int x^p y^q f(x/\alpha, y/\beta) dx dy$$
$$= \int \int (\alpha x)^p (\beta y)^q f(x, y) \alpha \beta dx dy = \alpha^{p+1} \beta^{q+1} m_{pq}$$

If we take $\gamma = \alpha = \beta$, normalizing the moments by m_{00}^γ, where $\gamma = (p + q + 2)/2$, will make them size invariant:

$$\frac{m'_{pq}}{m_{00}'^{\gamma}} = \frac{\gamma^{2\gamma m_{pq}}}{(\gamma^2 m_{00})^\gamma}$$

Rotation: The rotation of f about its origin by an angle θ results in $f'(x, y) = f(x \cos \theta + y \sin \theta, -x \sin \theta + y \cos \theta)$. The rotated moment is given by [22, 119]:

$$m'_{pq} = \sum \sum (x \cos \theta + y \sin \theta)^p (y \cos \theta - x \sin \theta)^q f(x, y)$$

Reflection: A reflection about the y-axis results in a change of sign of all moments that depend on the power of y. The reflected moment is given by [22, 119]:

$$m'_{pq} = \int \int x^p y^q f(x, -y) dx dy = (-1)^q m_{pq}$$

In a similar fashion we can find reflection moment for the x-axis.

Hu's Absolute Orthogonal Moment Invariants

In 1962, on the bases of the second and third order normalized central moments Hu proposed a set of seven moments invariant to orientation, position and size changes, also known as *Absolute Similitude Moment Invariants* [17]:

$$\phi_1 = \eta_{20} + \eta_{02}$$
$$\phi_2 = (\eta_{20} - \eta_{02})^2 + 4\eta_{11}^2$$

$$\phi_3 = (\eta_{30} - 3\eta_{12})^2 + (3\eta_{21} - \eta_{03})^2$$
$$\phi_4 = (\eta_{30} + \eta_{12})^2 + (\eta_{21} + \eta_{03})^2$$
$$\phi_5 = (\eta_{30} - 3\eta_{12})(\eta_{30} + \eta_{12})[(\eta_{30} + \eta_{21})^2 - 3(\eta_{21} - \eta_{03})^2]$$
$$+ (3\eta_{21} - \eta_{03})(\eta_{21} + \eta_{03})[3(\eta_{30} + \eta_{12})^2 - (\eta_{21} + \eta_{03})^2]$$
$$\phi_6 = (\eta_{20} - \eta_{02})[(\eta_{30} + \eta_{12})^2 - (\eta_{21} - \eta_{03})^2] + 4\eta_{11}(\eta_{30} + \eta_{12})(\eta_{21} + \eta_{03})$$
$$\phi_7 = (3\eta_{21} - \eta_{03})(\eta_{30} + \eta_{12})[(\eta_{30} + \eta_{12})^2 - 3(\eta_{21} - \eta_{03})^2]$$
$$- (\eta_{30} - 3\eta_{12})(\eta_{21} + \eta_{03})[3(\eta_{30} + \eta_{12})^2 - (\eta_{21} + \eta_{03})^2]$$

In addition, $\phi_1...\phi_6$ are also invariant to reflection, and ϕ_7 changes sign under the mirroring operation.

Hu's moments are some of the most popular moment invariants in pattern recognition and have been studied for years. As a result, multiple problems with them have been discovered [119]:

- ϕ_6 and ϕ_7 may be several orders of magnitude greater than ϕ_1 and ϕ_2, making classification more complicated.

- Since it can be shown that, $\phi_7^2 + \phi_5^2 = \phi_4^3$, there are actually only six independent Hu's moments.

- In relation to grayscale images, Hu's moments are not invariant to contrast changes.

Some attempts at resolving above-mentioned problems have been reported [119]:

- Maitra proposed a set of six moments, which are invariant to contrast changes:

$$\beta_1 = \frac{\sqrt{\phi_2}}{\phi_1}, \ \beta_2 = \frac{\phi_3 \mu_{00}}{\phi_1 \phi_2}, \ \beta_3 = \frac{\phi_4}{\phi_3}, \ \beta_4 = \frac{\sqrt{\phi_5}}{\phi_4}, \ \beta_5 = \frac{\phi_6}{\phi_1 \phi_4}, \ \beta_6 = \frac{\phi_4}{\phi_3}$$

- Also in order to address contrast change invariants, Abozaid used a different normalization factor for the computation of Normalized Central

Moments:

$$\eta'_{pq} = \frac{\mu_{pq}}{\mu_{00}} \left(\frac{\mu_{00}}{\mu_{20} + \mu_{02}} \right)^{(p+q)/2}$$

Affine Moment Invariants

Proposed by Flusser et al. [49, 50, 51] *Affine Moment Invariants* (AMI) are derived by means of general theory of algebraic invariants. The AMIs are invariant under general affine transformations [49]:

$$u = a_0 + a_1 x + a_2 y \qquad v = b_0 + b_1 x + b_2 y$$

where (x, y) and (u, v) are coordinates in the image plane before and after the transformation, respectively. Below we provide three simplest AMIs as given in [49]

$$I_1 = \frac{1}{\mu_{00}^4} (\mu_{20} \mu_{02} - \mu_{11}^2)$$

$$I_2 = \frac{1}{\mu_{00}^{10}} (\mu_{30}^2 \mu_{03}^2 - 6\mu_{30} \mu_{21} \mu_{12} \mu_{03} - 4\mu_{30} \mu_{12}^2 + 4\mu_{30} \mu_{12}^3 + 4\mu_{03} \mu_{21}^3 - 3\mu_{21}^2 \mu_{12}^2)$$

$$I_3 = \frac{1}{\mu_{00}^7} (\mu_{20} (\mu_{21} \mu_{03} - \mu_{12}^2) - \mu_{11} (\mu_{30} \mu_{03} - \mu_{21} \mu_{12}) + \mu_{02} (\mu_{30} \mu_{12} - \mu_{21}^2))$$

Interested reader is encouraged to read original papers by Flusser et al. [49, 50, 51] for detailed derivation of AMIs as well as proofs and explicitly calculated higher order moments.

Blur Moment Invariants

Much work in pattern recognition has been devoted to finding features invariant to changes in location, scale in rotation. Flusser et al. [49, 50, 51] have developed a moment based feature, which is aimed at fighting another type of transformation, so called image *blurring*. Blurring can be caused by an out-of-focus camera, vibrations, or sensor motion [49]. The blur moments have the following definition:
If $(p + q)$ is even, then:

$$C(p, q) = 0$$

65

If $(p + q)$ is odd, then:

$$C(p, q) = \mu_{pq} - \frac{1}{\mu_{00}} \sum_{n=0}^{p} \sum_{\substack{M=0 \\ o < n+m < p+q}}^{q} \binom{p}{n} \binom{q}{m} C(p-n, q-m)\mu_{nm}$$

Using the above definition, and applying a specially developed for that purpose algorithm, Flusser et al. [51] propose the following low-order motion blur invariants:
Zeroth order:

$$m_0 = \mu_{00}$$

Second order:

$$m_1 = \mu_{11}$$

$$m_2 = \mu_{02}$$

Third order:

$$m_3 = \mu_{12}$$

$$m_4 = \mu_{21}$$

$$m_5 = \mu_{03}$$

$$m_6 = \mu_{30}$$

Fourth order:

$$m_7 = \mu_{04}$$

$$m_8 = \mu_{13}$$

$$m_9 = \mu_{22} - \frac{\mu_{20}\mu_{02}}{\mu_{00}}$$

$$m_{10} = \mu_{31} - \frac{3\mu_{20}\mu_{11}}{\mu_{00}}$$

Original paper lists twenty additional blur invariant moments up to the seventh order [51].

Affine and Blur Moment Invariants

Since both Affine and Blur Moment Invariants were proposed by Flusser et al. [49, 50, 51], it was only natural for them to combine both types of moments into a single invariant feature they, not surprisingly, call *Combined*

Blur-Affine Invariants (CBAI). The main goal of this development was to combine invariant properties of both types, to achieve a true level of deformation invariants in the feature.

Both derivation and its proof can be found in [49] and are somewhat complicated. Just to illustrate the simplest CBAI in explicit form is:

$$I_1 = (\mu_{30}^2\mu_{03}^2 - 6\mu_{30}\mu_{21}\mu_{12}\mu_{03} + 4\mu_{30}\mu_{12}^3 + 4\mu_{21}^3 - 3\mu_{21}^2\mu_{12}^2)/\mu_{00}^{10}$$

and they only get exponentially more complicated. Clearly, as it is beyond the scope of this book to list all known moments and their invariants, we will simple direct an interested reader towards the original paper of Flusser et al. [49, 50, 51]

2.4.4 Radial and Angular Moments

If $g(r, \theta)$ represents the image function in polar coordinates, then the *Radial* and *Angular* moments are defined as follows [38, 119]:

$$\psi_r(k, g) = \int_r r^k g(r, \theta) dr$$

$$\psi_\theta(p, q, g) = \int_\theta \cos^p(\theta) \sin^q(\theta) g(r, \theta) d\theta$$

$$\psi(k, p, q, g) = \int_r \int_\theta r^k g(r, \theta) \cos^p(\theta) \sin^q(\theta) d\theta dr$$

In case of digital images, we can say:

$$\psi(k, p, q, g) = \sum_r \sum_\theta r^k g(r, \theta) \cos^p(\theta) \sin^q(\theta)$$

The assumption is made that the image is located around its centroid.

Use of Radial and Angular moments for character recognition can be observed in works of Desai [38] and Maurycy [119]. For example, Desai combines this approach with image segmentation into Tracks and Sectors (see Section 2.2.6 for details). In this approach, the first order radial moment of the segment contained between angles α and $\alpha + \beta$ and band between circles of radius r_j and r_{j+1} is given by:

$$\psi^i = \psi^{(r_j, s_\alpha)}(1, g) = \sum_{r_j}^{r_{j+1}} \sum_{\alpha}^{\alpha+\beta} rg(r, \theta)$$

where $i = j_n + \frac{\alpha}{\beta} + 1$ and $\beta = \frac{360^\circ}{n}$

2.4.5 Gegenbauer Moments

Many newly developed orthogonal moments are based on a particular family of orthogonal polynomials. In particular, *Gegenbauer* Moments are based on Gegenbauer Polynomials (GP), which are a class of orthogonal polynomials on the interval $[-1, 1]$. GPs are characterized by a single parameter λ that determines the form of the polynomial. So, $G_n(x; \lambda)$ denotes Gegebauer polynomials of order n with the parameter λ restricted to $\lambda > -.5$ [30, 102].

The GP system is related to another family of polynomials, namely Jacobi polynomials $P_n^{(a,b)}(x)$ by the following equation:

$$G_n(x; \lambda) = \frac{\Gamma(\lambda + .5)}{\Gamma(2\lambda)} \frac{\Gamma(n + 2\lambda)}{\Gamma(n + \lambda + .5)} P_n^{(\lambda - .5, \lambda - .5)}(x)$$

where $\Gamma(x)$ is the Gamma function. It is interesting to observe that if $\lambda = .5$, $G_n(x; .5)$ becomes the Legendre polynomial (see Section 2.4.6 for more information of Legendre polynomials and moments) [30, 102].

The Gegenbauer moment $A_n(\lambda)$ is given by

$$A_n(\lambda) = c_n(\lambda) \int_{-1}^{1} f(t) G_n(t; \lambda)(1 - t^2)^{(\lambda - .5)} dt$$

where C_n is the normalizing constant expressed as:

$$C_n(\lambda) = \frac{2^{2\lambda} \Gamma^2(\lambda)}{2\pi} \frac{n!}{\Gamma(n + 2\lambda)}(n + \lambda)$$

where $\lambda \neq 0$ [30, 102].

In case of a two-dimensional image $f(x, y)$ we can define the (p, q) Gegenbauer moment as follows:

$$A_{p,q}(\lambda) = C_p(\lambda) \int_{-1}^{1} \int_{-1}^{1} f(u, v) G_p(u; \lambda)(1 - u^2)^{(\lambda - .5)} (1 - v^2)^{(\lambda - .5)} du dv$$

where $\lambda > -\frac{1}{2}$.

In their research in Chinese character recognition, Chiang et al. [30, 102], developed a four dimensional feature vector based on lower order Gegenbauer moments. The definitions for all four feature-vector elements used by them are presented below:

$$f_1 = A_{2,0}(\lambda) + A_{0,2}(\lambda)$$
$$f_2 = \sqrt{(A_{2,0}(\lambda) - A_{0,2}(\lambda))^2 + 4A_{1,1}(\lambda)}$$
$$f_3 = \sqrt{(A_{3,0}(\lambda) - 3A_{1,2}(\lambda))^2 + (3A_{2,1}(\lambda) - A_{0,3}(\lambda))^2}$$
$$f_4 = A_{3,0}(\lambda) + A_{0,3}(\lambda)$$

Their research also showed that in general, Gegenbauer moments with smaller λs have higher recognition power. Also, as was aforementioned when $\lambda = .5$, Gegenbauer polynomials become Legendre polynomials. This means that Moments extracted from Gegenbauer polynomials have much greater recognition power than those based on Legendre moments (see Section 2.4.6 on Legendre moments) [30, 102].

2.4.6 Legendre Moments

The use of Legendre moments was proposed by Teaque [142] and later investigated as a feature used in recognition of Chinese, Farsi and English characters, Arabic and Farsi numerals and even simple images [6, 36, 101, 103, 104, 112, 141, 150]. The Legendre moments are defined as [21]:

$$\lambda_{pq} = \frac{(2p + 1)(2q + 1)}{4} \int_{-\infty}^{\infty} \int_{-\infty}^{\infty} P_p(x) P_q(y) f(x, y) dx dy$$

in case of digital images:

$$\lambda_{pq} = \frac{(2p+1)(2q+1)}{(M-1)(N-1)} \sum_{x=0}^{M-1} \sum_{y=0}^{N-1} P_p(x)P_q(y)f(x,y)$$

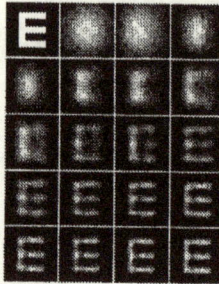

Figure 2.29: Reconstruction of the letter 'E' by Legendre moments. From top to bottom row and left to right in each row: original input image, reconstructed image with up to second order moment through up to twentieth order moment [32].

The Legendre polynomials $\{P_p(x)\}$ are a complete orthogonal basis set on the interval $[-1, 1]$:

$$\int_{-1}^{1} P_p(x)P_q(y)dx = \frac{2}{2p+1}\delta_{pq}$$

The nth order Legendre polynomial is defined by:

$$P_q(x) = \frac{1}{2^q} \sum_{p=0}^{q/2} (-1)^m \frac{(2q-2p)!}{p!(q-p)!(q-2p)!} x^{q-2p}$$

or more simply

$$P_q(x) = \sum_{k=0}^{q} Cqkx^k$$

where the Legendre coefficients are given by:

$$C_{qk} = (-1)^{(q-k)/2} \frac{(k+q)!}{2[(q-k)/2]![(k+q)/2]!k!}$$

if $q - k$ is even, and is zero otherwise.

Figure 2.29 shows reconstruction abilities of Legendre moments as applied to capital letter 'E'.

2.4.7 Tchebichef Moments

Tchebichef (sometimes referred to as Chebyshev) moments (TM), unlike Zernike and Legendre moments, belong to the class of discrete orthogonal moments [199]. As the result, the implementation of these moments does not involve any numerical approximation or coordinate space transformations [200].

Tchebichef moments are based on discrete orthogonal Tchebichef polynomials satisfying

$$\sum_{x=0}^{N-1} t_p(x)t_q x = \rho(p, N)\delta_{nm}$$

where the set of discrete classical Tchebichef polynomials is defined by

$$t_n(x) = n! \sum_{x=0}^{n} (-1)^{n-k} \begin{pmatrix} N-1-k \\ n-k \end{pmatrix} \begin{pmatrix} n+k \\ n \end{pmatrix} \begin{pmatrix} x \\ k \end{pmatrix}$$

The Tchebichef polynomials satisfy the property of orthogonality, with

$$\rho(p, N) = (2n)! \begin{pmatrix} N+n \\ 2n+1 \end{pmatrix} = \frac{N(N^2 - 1)...(N^2 - n^2)}{2n + 1}$$

for the image represented by $f(x, y)$, the Tchebichef moment with order $(n + m)$ is defined by

$$T_{nm} = \frac{1}{\rho(n, N)\rho(m, N)} \sum_{x=0}^{N-1} \sum_{y=0}^{N-1} t_n(x)t_m(y)f(x, y)$$

where $p, q \in [0, N-1]$ and t_n is the basis set. The inverse moment transform can be used to reconstruct the original image and is given by:

$$f(x,y) = \sum_{m=0}^{N-1} \sum_{n=0}^{N-1} T_{mn} t_m(x) t_n(y)$$

if the moment is limited to the $\leq P$ order, then $f(x,y)$ can be approximated by

$$f(x,y) = \sum_{n=0}^{P} \sum_{m=0}^{n} T_{n-m,m} t_{n-m}(x) t_n(y)$$

Original Image	Reconstructed Images							
E								
Recn. Error:	64	26	14	3	2	2	0	0
			Using Tchebichef Moments					
Recn. Error:	50	31	25	6	7	3	1	1
			Using Legendre Moments					
Recn. Error:	73	64	68	52	42	21	11	2
			Using Zernike Moments					
Maximum Order of Moments	7	8	9	10	11	12	13	14

Figure 2.30: Reconstruction of the letter 'E' by Tchebichef, Legendre and Zernike moments, with reconstruction error shown [130].

Certain properties of TM make them particularly attractive as feature representing moments. Symmetry property can be used to significantly reduce the required computation time for Tchebichef moments. The scaled Tchebichef polynomials have the same symmetry property as the classical Tchebichef polynomials:

$$t_n(N - 1 - x) = (-1)^n t_n(x)$$

This relation allows the subdivision of the domain of the original image into four equal parts and performing the computation of the polynomials only in the first quadrant. In addition to significantly reducing the computation time the symmetry property is also useful in minimizing storage space needed for TM.

Another attractive property of TM is the possibility of writing TM in terms of geometric moments as follows:

$$T_{pq} = A_p A_q \sum_{k=0}^{P} C_k(p, N) \sum_{\iota=0}^{q} C_\iota(q, N) \times \sum_{i=0}^{k} \sum_{j=0}^{\iota} s_k^{(i)} s_\iota^{(j)} m_{ij}$$

where

$$A_p = \frac{1}{\beta(p, N)\rho(p, N)}$$

It is obvious that TM depend on the geometric moments up to the same order. The explicit representation of the TM in terms of the geometric moments up to the second order is given bellow:

$$T_{00} = \frac{m_{00}}{N^2}$$

$$T_{10} = \frac{6m_{10} + 3(1 - N)m_{00}}{N(N^2 - 1)}$$

$$T_{01} = \frac{6m_{01} + 3(1 - N)m_{00}}{N(N^2 - 1)}$$

$$T_{20} = \frac{30m_{20} + 30(1 - N)m_{10} + 5(1 - N)(2 - N)m_{00}}{(N^2 - 1)(N^2 - 4)}$$

$$T_{02} = \frac{30m_{02} + 30(1 - N)m_{01} + 5(1 - N)(2 - N)m_{00}}{(N^2 - 1)(N^2 - 4)}$$

$$T_{11} = \frac{36m_{11} + 18(1 - N)(m_{10} + m_{01}) + 9(1 - N)^2 m_{00}}{(N^2 - 1)^2}$$

In practical experiments, TM are most often compared against Zernike and Legendre moments and are shown to be effective feature descriptors, with superior feature representation capability [130]. Figures 2.30, 2.31, 2.32

demonstrate superior performance (via reconstruction) of TM as compared
to Zernike and Legendre moments.

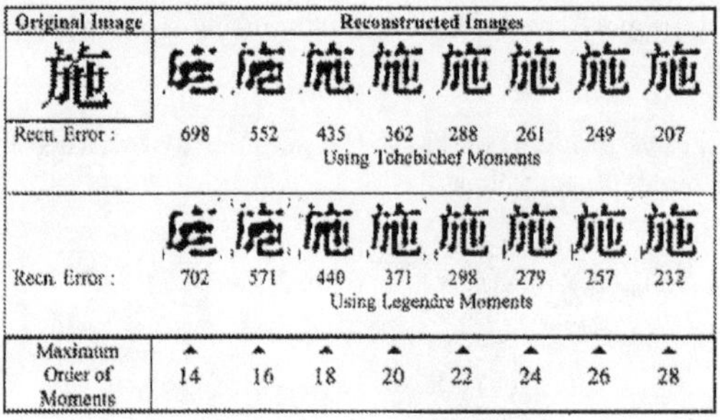

Original Image	Reconstructed Images							
施	施	施	施	施	施	施	施	施
Recn. Error :	698	552	435	362	288	261	249	207
	Using Tchebichef Moments							
Recn. Error :	702	571	440	371	298	279	257	232
	Using Legendre Moments							
Maximum Order of Moments	14	16	18	20	22	24	26	28

Figure 2.31: Reconstruction of the Chinese character by higher order
Tchebichef and Legendre moments with reconstruction error shown [130].

Original Image	Original Image With Noise							
要	要							
	Reconstructed Images							
Recn. Error :	614	552	493	429	331	301	290	262
	Using Tchebichef Moments							
Recn. Error :	640	576	537	457	417	378	366	361
	Using Legendre Moments							
Maximum Order of Moments	14	16	18	20	22	24	26	28

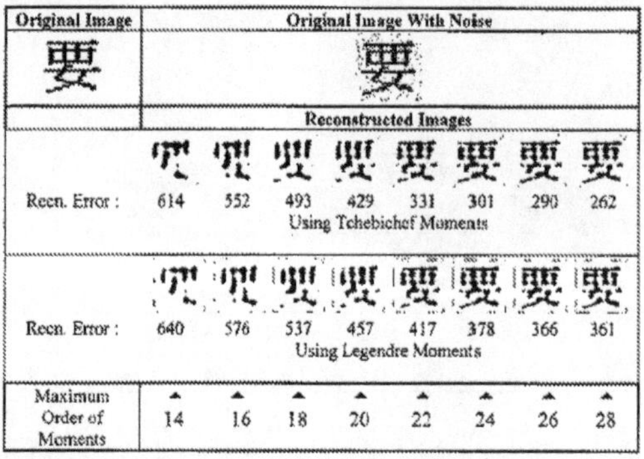

Figure 2.32: Reconstruction of the Chinese character by higher order
Tchebichef and Legendre moments with reconstruction error shown [130].

2.4.8   Krawtchouk Moments

Originally introduced for image reconstruction by Yap at al. [198], Krawtchouk moments (KM) have also been utilized as pattern descriptors [201]. KM are based on orthogonal Krawtchouk polynomials satisfying:

$$\sum_{x=0}^{N} j(x)k_n(x)k_n(x) = \rho(N,n,p)\delta_{pq} \ 0 \le m,n \le N$$

where

$$\rho(N,n,p) = \binom{N}{n} p^n(1-p)^n$$

The hypergeometric representation of the Krawtchouk polynomial is given by:

$$k_n(x) = q^n \binom{x}{n} F\left(-n, x-N; x-n; -\frac{p}{q}\right)$$

with the weight function being:

$$j(x) = \binom{N}{x} p^x q^{N-x}$$

Krawtchouk moments like Tchebichef moments are discrete orthogonal moments and so unlike Zernike or Legendre moments do not require any numerical approximation in their computation. Furthermore, KM do not require coordinate space transformations [198]. KM of order $n+m$ is given by:

$$k_{nm} = [\rho(N,n,p)\rho(N,m,p)]^{-1} \sum_{x=0}^{N-1}\sum_{y=0}^{N-1} j(x)k_n(x)j(y)k_m(y)f(x,y)$$

where $n,m = 0,1,2,...N$ The inverse moment transform is used to reconstruct the image and is given by:

$$f(x,y) = \sum_{m=0}^{N}\sum_{n=0}^{N} K_{nm}k_n(x)k_m(y)$$

In their experiments Yap et al. [198] compared KM with Tchebichef, Zernike and Legendre moments with results demonstrating superior performance of KM with respect to image reconstruction and concluded that they would be ideally suited for image processing. KM required as little as twenty moments for an acceptable level image reconstruction.

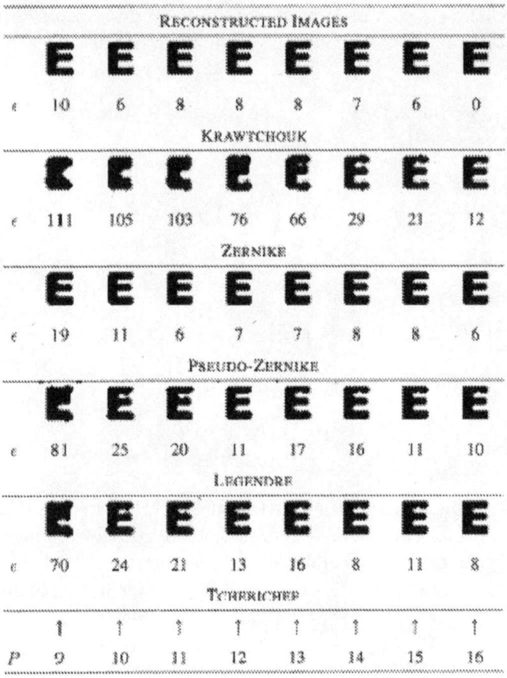

Figure 2.33: Reconstruction of the letter 'E' by Tchebichef, Legendre, Zernike, Pseudo-Zernike and Krawtchouk moments of orders 9 through 16, with reconstruction error shown [201].

Figure 2.33 demonstrates a superior performance of KM, as a result of them being able to represent sharp edges even at the lower moments, a property inherited from lower order weighted Krawtchouk polynomials, which have relatively high spatial frequency components. Later on, Yap et al. [201] compared KM with Hu's invariants in the pattern recognition task and once again concluded that KM provided a better alternative in terms of accuracy.

2.4.9   Zernike Moments

Khotanzad et al. [87, 88] proposed using Zernike moments (ZM) for image recognition. ZM are based on Zernike complex polynomials, which form a complete orthogonal set over unit disk $x^2 + y^2 \leq 1$. They are expressed by [88, 150]:

$$V_{nm}(x,y) = V_{nm}(\rho,\theta) = R_{nm}(\rho)e^{jm\theta}$$

where $n \geq 0$, $|m| \leq n$, $n - |m|$ even, $\rho = \sqrt{x^2 + y^2}$, $\theta = tan^{-1}(y/x)$, $\jmath = \sqrt{-1}$, and:

$$R_{nm}(x,y) = R_{nm}(\rho) = \sum_{s=0}^{(n-|m|)/2} (-1)^s \frac{(n-s)!}{s!((n-|m|)/2 - s)!((n+|m|)/2 - s)!}\rho^{n-2s}$$

These polynomials are orthogonal and satisfy [119]:

$$\int\int_{x^2+y^2\leq 1} V_{nm}^*(x,y)dxdy = \frac{\pi}{n+1}\delta_{np}\delta_{mq}$$

where $\delta_{ab} = 1$ if $a = b$ and 0 otherwise.

Figure 2.34: Reconstruction of the letter 'E' by Zernike moments. From top to bottom row and left to right in each row: original input image, reconstructed image with second order moment through up to twentieth order moment [32].

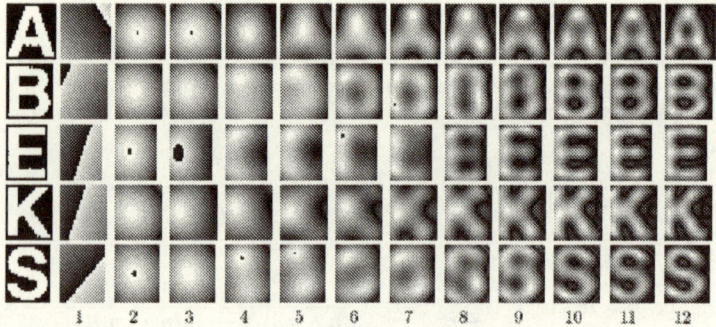

Figure 2.35: Examples of letters reconstructed with Zernike moments up to the twelfth order [119].

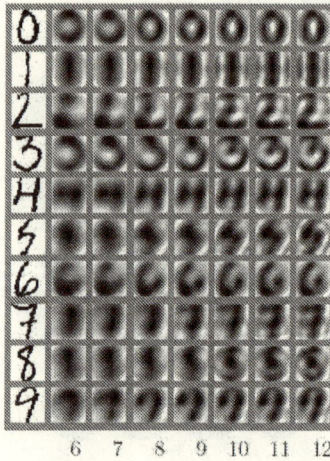

Figure 2.36: Examples of digits reconstructed with Zernike moments up to the twelve order [94].

Zernike moments are the projection of the image function $f(x, y)$ onto these orthogonal basis functions. The ZM of order $n + m$ is given by:

$$A_{nm} = \frac{n+1}{\pi} \int\int_{x^2+y^2 \leq 1} f(x,y)V_{nm}^*(\rho, \theta)dxdy$$

In the case of a discrete digital image we get:

$$A_{nm} = \frac{n+1}{\pi} \sum_x \sum_y f(x,y)V_{nm}^*(\rho, \theta)$$

keeping $x^2 + y^2 \leq 1$ and with symbol $*$ denoting the complex conjugate operator.

For computing of ZM of a given image, the center of the image is taken to be the origin and pixel coordinates are mapped to the range of unit circle. The pixels falling outside that range are not used in the computation. The original image inside the unit circle can be reconstructed using:

$$f(x,y) = \lim_{N \to \infty} \sum_{n=0}^{N} \sum_m A_{nm}V_{nm}(x,y)$$

where the second sum is taken over all $|m| \leq n$, such that $n - |m|$ is even. Figures 2.34, 2.35 and 2.36 demonstrate reconstructive ability of Zernike moments up to the twelve order.

Zernike moments could be expressed in terms of polar coordinates by changing the integration variables:

$$A_{nm} = \frac{n+1}{\pi} \int_0^{2\pi} \int_0^1 f(r,\theta)V_{nm}^*(r, \theta)rdrd\theta$$

with $x = r\cos\theta$ and $y = r\sin\theta$. This form can be utilized for derivation of moments of a rotated image $f^r(r, \theta) = f(r, \theta - \alpha)$ by an angle α. We get [94]:

$$A_{nm}^r = \frac{n+1}{\pi} \int_0^{2\pi} \int_0^1 f(r, \theta - \alpha)R_{nm}(\rho)e^{-jm\theta}rdrd\theta = e^{-jm\alpha}A_{nm}$$

2.4.10   Pseudo-Zernike Moments

A set of orthogonal polynomials related to Zernike Polynomials (ZP) is the so-called set of Pseudo-Zernike polynomials with properties similar to those of traditional ZP. The main difference is that Pseudo-Zernike polynomials are defined not just in x, y but also in r as [32]:

$$R_{nm}(x, y) = R_{nm}(r) = \sum_{s=0}^{n-|m|} (-1)^s \frac{(2n+1-s)!}{s!(n-|m|-s)!(n+|m|+1-s)!} r^{n-s}$$

The Pseudo-Zernike moments (PZM) are then defined by:

$$P_{nm} = \frac{n+1}{\pi} \sum_x \sum_y f(x, y) R_{nm}(x, y) e^{-jm\theta}$$

where $n \geq 0$ and $|m| \leq n$, while the condition '$n - |m|$ is even' has been relaxed [119]. As a result, there are approximately twice as many Pseudo-Zernike moments as there are conventional Zernike moments.

The set of Pseudo-Zernike polynomials contains $(n+1)^2$ linearly independent polynomials of degree $\leq n$, whereas the set of Zernike polynomials contains only $\frac{(n+1)(n+2)}{2}$ linearly independent polynomials of degree $\leq n$ [32].

PZN are less sensitive to image noise as compared to the conventional Zernike moments and have a wider dynamic range. PZM of functions have the same form and same rotational properties as ZM. Figures 2.37 and 2.38 demonstrate reconstructive abilities of Pseudo-Zernike moments up to the twelfth order. Figure 2.38 could be compared with figure 2.35, which shows similar reconstruction using Zernike moments. Clearly, PZM outperform traditional Zernike moments for all cases demonstrated.

If desired, PZM can be computed in terms of the scale invariant Central moments and the Radial-Geometric moments which are given as [36]:

$$H_{pq} = \sum_x \sum_y f(x, y)(x^2 + y^2)^{1/2} x^p y^q$$

Figure 2.37: Reconstruction of the letter 'E' by Pseudo-Zernike moments. From top to bottom row and left to right in each row: original input image, reconstructed image with up to second order moment through up to twentieth order moment [32].

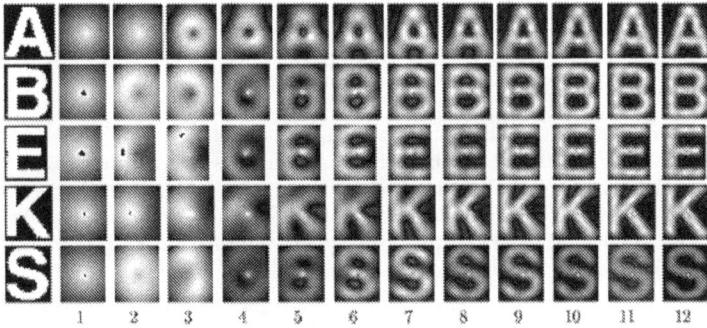

Figure 2.38: Examples of letters reconstructed with Pseudo-Zernike moments up to the twelfth order [119].

2.4.11 Fourier-Mellon Moments

Heavily researched by Hew [64, 65, 66, 67, 68], orthogonal Fourier-Mellon moments (FMM) are similar to Zernike moments. They have the same invariants properties with respect to scale, rotation and translation of the image. The Orthogonal Fourier-Mellon basis function is given by:

$$U_{pq}(\rho, \theta) = Q_p(\rho)e^{jq\theta}$$

where $p \geq 0$, q is an integer and (ρ, θ) is the radial-polar form of (x, y). $Q_p(\rho)$ is the radial polynomial given by:

$$Q_p(\rho) = \sum_{s=0}^{p} \frac{(-1)^s(2p + 1 - s)!}{s!(p - s)!(p + 1 - s)!}\rho^{p-s}$$

It follows that a Fourier-Mellon moment of order $p + q$ is given by:

$$M_{pq} = \frac{p + 1}{\pi}U_{pq}$$

Unlike with Zernike moments, for FMM there is no restrictions on q from p, so there is no natural count on the number of non-redundant moments. As a result of the behavior of Fourier-Mellon basis functions under conjugation, one can make a big improvement in computation time required, by not calculating redundant moments of the image. Unlike with the ZM or Pseudo-ZM, FMM can't be expressed in terms of geometric moments [66].

Figures 2.39 and 2.39 demonstrate reconstructive abilities of FMM on two English characters, namely 'b' and 'h'. As can be seen from the images, a very large number of FMM is required for a recognizable quality reproduction of the original image to be reconstructed. But this is exactly the quality of reconstruction we are looking for if we are to believe that FMM capture all the necessary information of as Hew himself puts it in [68]:

> We seek the moments which best record the structure perceived by the human eye-brain combination. We must therefore assess moment sets by visual inspection of reconstructed images; if a human cannot recognize the digit in a given reconstruction, then moments which generated it did not capture the appropriate details.

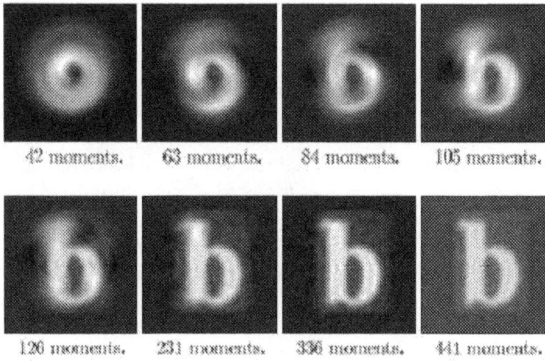

Figure 2.39: Reconstruction of the letter 'b' by Fourier-Mellon moments. Reconstructed image with up to 441 moments [66].

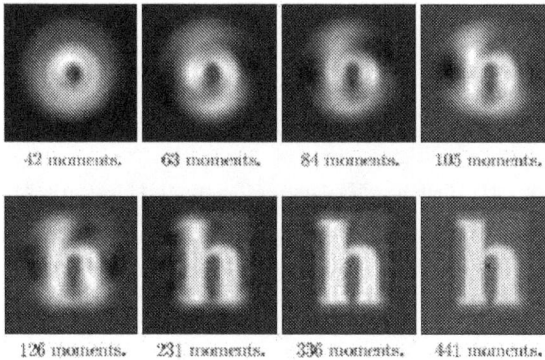

Figure 2.40: Reconstruction of the letter 'h' by Fourier-Mellon moments. Reconstructed image with up to 441 moments [66].

2.5   Structural Approaches

2.5.1   Structural Features

This is a high-level feature, which is partially inspired by the way humans process patterns. Instead of describing an image in terms of individual pixels or their statistical groupings, general shape of an object is used as a feature, so it is also referred to as *Discrete Features*. For example the number of loops, junctions, crossings, and end points are used to classify patterns [132, 186]. The coordinates and other additional descriptions of these entities may be included. Figure 2.41 demonstrates structural features, which can be used to properly classify digit '6'. For this feature extraction method to succeed, an important processing step - image thinning is a must, since a character skeleton is needed for high accuracy performance [119].

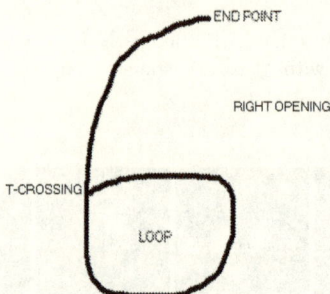

Figure 2.41: Digit six with some of its structural features shown.

The biggest problem with the structural feature extraction approach is the actual extraction of the feature. While it is extremely easy for humans to pick out such elements of the pattern as holes and crossing, it is really challenging to accurately do so in a computer algorithm. Many different approaches exist, but the actual implementation is irrelevant as long as it produces structural elements of the pattern as its output. Many features listed in this book are potential structural feature extractors. For example, Hough transform (see Section 2.6.3) is often used to detect loops or circles in images.

Typically a decision tree classifier is used with this feature [144]. Given a description of the pattern in terms of its structural elements it is capable of pinpointing with high accuracy the type of the pattern is being examined. This is especially effective within small groups of structurally diverse patterns, such as digits. Figure 2.42 shows just such a decision tree used by Lee at al. [97] to preclassify a subset of digits, the other digits are later classified using a Hopfield neural network.

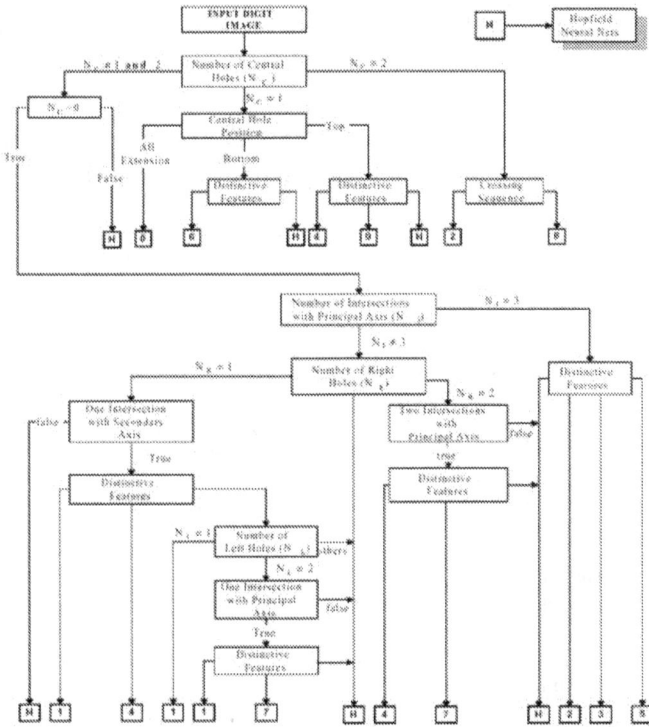

Figure 2.42: Decision tree for numerical images [97].

2.5.2 Feature Points

A type of structural (See section 2.5.1) feature, Feature Points (FP) or *Fork* points as they are sometimes called are very popular, particularly in Asian character recognition [54, 108, 109], but they are also used with other alphabets [40, 71, 85]. FP represent places of interest in the pattern. Those are locations at which significant structural changes take place in the image. Feature points can also assist in decomposition of large strokes into smaller segments. Examples of those include intersections of two or more strokes, end points of strokes as well as corner points made up by two strokes touching at their ends. Figure 2.43 shows FP from 1-fork to 6-fork along with their conventional names. Figure 2.45 demonstrates examples of characters with certain feature point configurations.

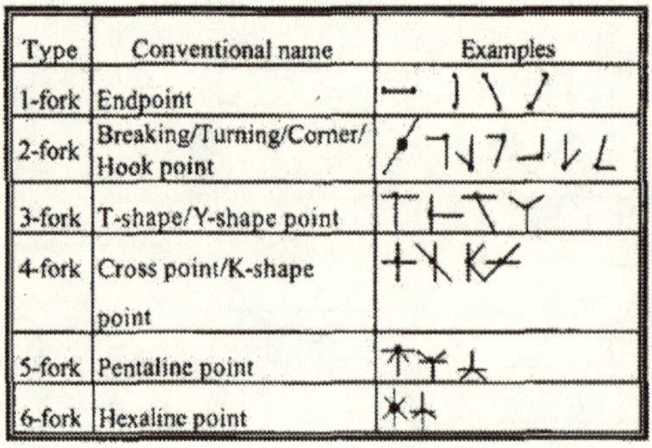

Type	Conventional name	Examples
1-fork	Endpoint	
2-fork	Breaking/Turning/Corner/ Hook point	
3-fork	T-shape/Y-shape point	
4-fork	Cross point/K-shape point	
5-fork	Pentaline point	
6-fork	Hexaline point	

Figure 2.43: Basic point types with examples [165].

If feature points are not used to improve recognition of strokes in the pattern, they are used as a set to describe a pattern and classify it based on such a description set. Different researchers often try to come up with an original definition of feature points, which they feel would allow for a highly descriptive set to represent an image. For example Hu et al. [71] propose the following definitions of feature points, which includes Directional and Bend points:

- Terminal point: a T point is the point, which has only one neighbor in its 8-neighborhood.

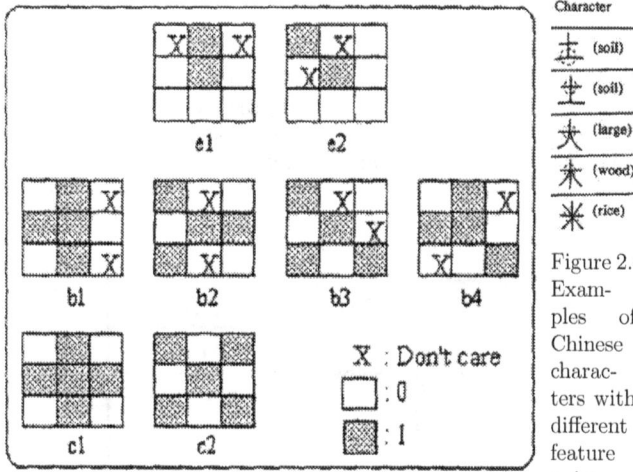

Figure 2.44: Templates used for extraction of feature points [44].

Figure 2.45: Examples of Chinese characters with different feature points shown [206].

- Intersection point: an I point is the point which has at least three neighbors in its 8-neighborhood.

- Directional point: a D point is the point at which a branch goes from one direction to its opposite direction horizontally or vertically.

- Bend point: a B point is the point at which the curvature of the curve is high. The detection of the B point is done by examining a number of consecutive points.

Once defined, a set of different points can be used to represent any pattern. Sometimes subdividing image into subzones and performing feature point extraction on each zones results in a more successful pattern description. The main challenge of FP feature is in locating the actual fork points. A straightforward way of doing so is by utilizing a set of simple masks configured to define different point types. An example of such feature point templates is shown in Figure 2.44.

2.5.3   Strokes

A type of structural feature closely associated with Feature Points (See Section 2.5.2), strokes are utilized particularly heavily in Asian character recognition [106, 124, 182, 188], Chinese being the most popular choice. This is mostly due to the fact that Asian characters are made primarily of individual strokes, also called radicals. While the combinations formed from multiple strokes can be very complex, any pattern in principle can be decomposed into just a few basic stroke types. The most commonly accepted basic strokes types are shown in the Figure 2.46 [2].

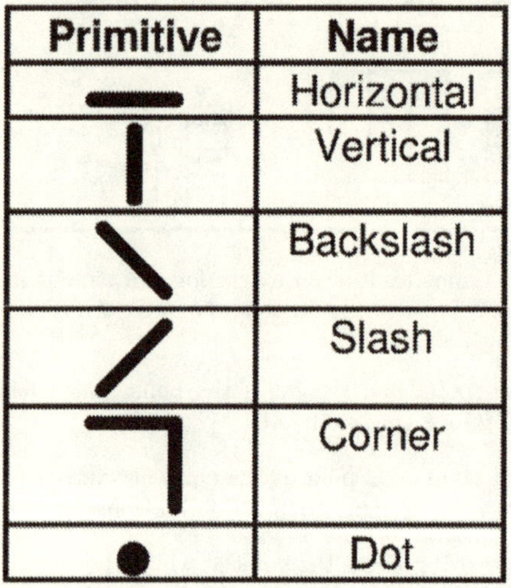

Primitive	Name
▬	Horizontal
❙	Vertical
＼	Backslash
／	Slash
┐	Corner
●	Dot

Figure 2.46: Basic types of strokes [2].

They are basically straight lines, drawn at four different angles, namely $0°$, $45°$, $90°$ and $135°$ as well as short stroke pattern called *dot*. Figure 2.47 shows same sample Asian characters along with four basic stroke types extracted from each [31]. A set of strokes of each type can be used as a feature vector component describing the original pattern. Total number of strokes of each type, as well as their locations and sizes can be used to further increase descriptive power of this feature.

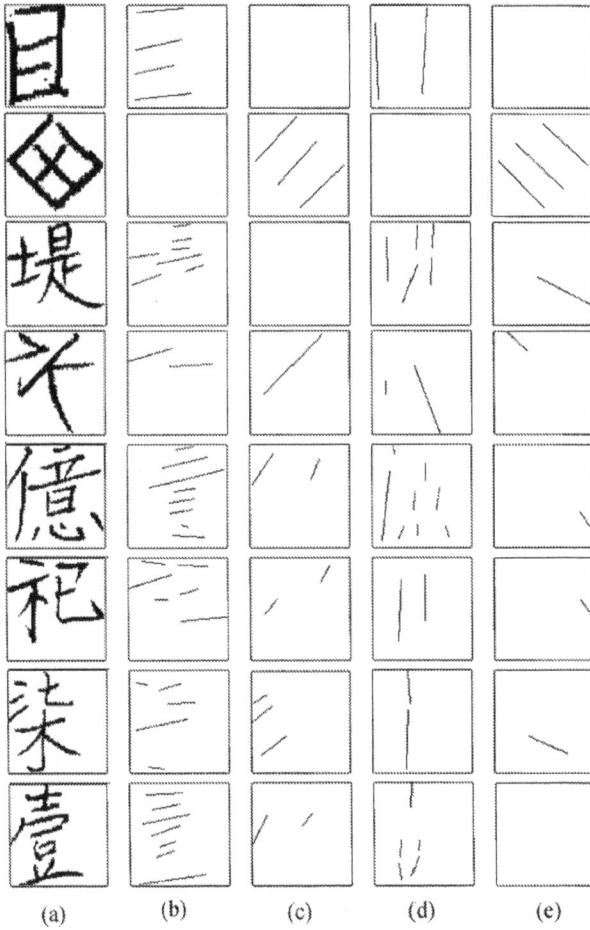

Figure 2.47: (a) Original characters; (b) Horizontal strokes; (c) Right-diagonal strokes; (d) Vertical strokes; (e) Left-diagonal strokes [31].

Many different stroke extraction techniques exist [121, 134, 140, 166], but most often the first step in extracting individual stokes from the pattern is to locate the Feature Points, which can be used to more accurately determine boundaries of, and relationships between the strokes. A preprocessing step of thinning is necessary to properly detect individual strokes, but as any pre-processing process it might result in the corruption of the original pattern and creation of ghost strokes or ghost feature points. A simple line-tracing algorithm can be used to detect the strokes afterward. As with any structural feature, extraction of the feature itself is the most challenging step with this approach.

In online character recognition, an additional ability of strokes to describe patterns can be derived from examining the relationships between neigh-boring or touching strokes. Figure 2.48 demonstrates some twelve different stroke relation types. Those relationships as a set can be used to improve overall discriminatory ability of the strokes feature and are not much harder to obtain than strokes themselves.

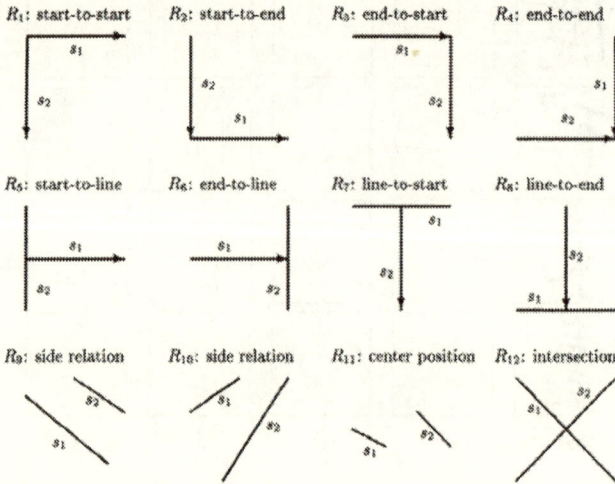

Figure 2.48: Inter-stroke relation types [107].

90

2.5.4 Character Profiles

One of the simplest in terms of both understanding and implementation is the *Character Profile* feature. Typically two (left and right) or four (left, right, up and down) character profiles are being extracted. The profiles give a measure of the variations of the shape on each side of the character [119]. Motivation for using just two profiles is that each half of the contour can be approximated by a discrete function of either x or y. Figure 2.49 demonstrates digit '5' and two discrete functions approximating its profiles from left and right [185].

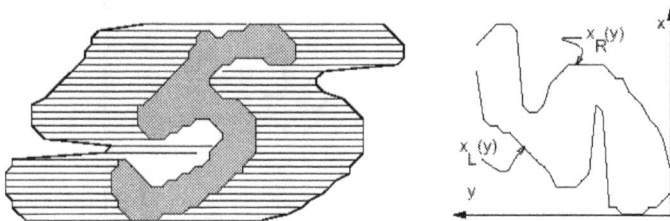

Figure 2.49: Digit '5' with left profile $X_L(y)$ and right profile $X_R(y)$. For each y value, the left (right) profile value is the leftmost (rightmost) x value on the character contour [185].

In some situations distinguishing between two different characters based on only two profiles is not feasible due to the similarity in shapes, as for example with handwritten digits '4' and '9'. In such a case, additional information is needed and it can be extracted from two additional sources, namely top and bottom profiles. Figure 2.50 demonstrates all four profiles for all Arabic digits as well as for some Latin characters [83].

Either outer or inner profiles may be extracted. To compute vertical profiles, we first locate the uppermost and lowermost points in the contour. The contour is split at these two points. To get the outer profiles for each y value, select the outermost x value on each contour half. To get the inner profiles for each y value, the innermost x value is chosen. Horizontal profiles

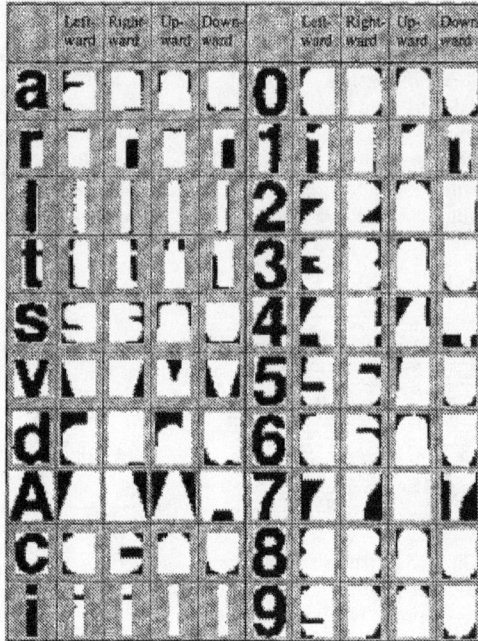

Figure 2.50: Left, Right, Lower and Upper profiles [83].

are computed in similar fashion, by dividing the contour into upper and lower halves.

Features Extracted From Character Profiles

The profiles can be used directly as feature vectors or processed further. Kimura et al. [89] proposed a series of additional features which can be extracted from the character profiles. Assuming that the left and right profiles are described by $LP(k)$ and $RP(k)$, where $k = 1, 2, ..., N$, the following additional global features can be computed:

The set of first differences of the left and right profiles:

$$LDIF(k) = LP(k) - LP(k-1), k = 2, 3, ..., N$$

$$RDIF(k) = RP(k) - RP(k-1), k = 2, 3, ..., N$$

Width equivalent feature:

$$W(k) = RP(k) - RP(k-1), k = 2, 3, ..., N$$

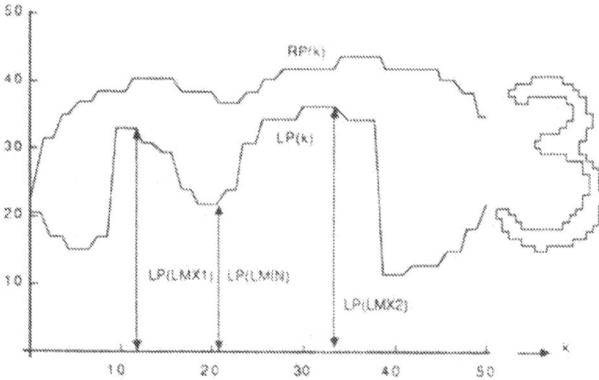

Figure 2.51: Maxima and Minima points on contour of digit '3' [89].

Local features are then defined for obtaining specific characterizations of the different patterns. The ratio is defined as:

$$Ratio = N/MAX_k(W(k))$$

Location of maxima and minima points is given as:

$$LMX = location\ of\ MAX_{R_1}(LP(k))$$

$$RMX = location\ of\ MAX_{R_1}(RP(k))$$

where R_1 is specified range within which LMX and RMX are evaluated. In a similar fashion we can define LMIN and RMIN [89].

An important feature in characterization of numerals according to Kimura et al. is the values of peaks in the first difference. These are defined as:

$$LPEAK^+ = MAX_{R_2}(LDIF(k))$$
$$LPEAK^- = MIN_{R_2}(LDIF(k))$$
$$RPEAK^+ = MAX_{R_2}(RDIF(k))$$
$$LPEAK^- = MIN_{R_2}(RDIF(k))$$
$$LPEAK = abs(LPEAK^+) + abs(LPEAK^-)$$
$$RPEAK = abs(RPEAK^+) + abs(RPEAK^-)$$

where R_2 is a specified range on $LDIF(k)$ or $RDIF(k)$. Figure 2.51 shows some of the additional features extracted by Kimura and his team from digit '3'.

Contour Sampling

Fu et al. [53] used an interesting oversimplification of the Profile feature. In his research, while trying to recognize Latin characters instead of taking the whole profile as a feature, Fu decided to utilize a sampling approach. Taking eight points around the character and finding the smallest distance to the contour of the pattern in order to get an $8D$ feature vector. Amazingly, the whole procedure was done MANUALY with the help of a ruler. Figure 2.52 visually demonstrates the approach taken by Fu and his team. While it is possible to implement this feature in software, it still would have limited discriminatory abilities and could only be utilized on relatively low in diversity pattern sets.

Peripheral Shape Features

Horizontal Peripheral Background Area (HPBA) and *Vertical Peripheral Background Area* (VPBA) features are utilized by Tang et al. [170] in their work on Chinese character recognition. While essentially they represent the same

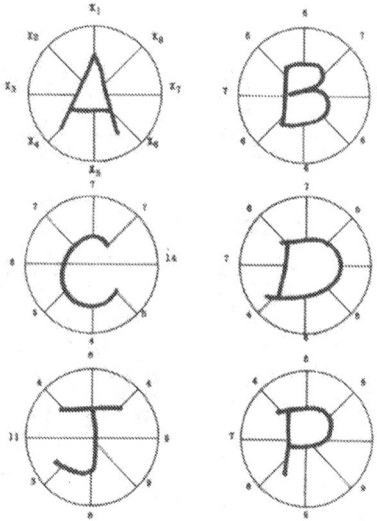

Figure 2.52: Contour profile sampling [53].

feature as Character Profiles, they provide a slightly different approach to thinking about this feature.

In order to find HPBA, the image is first subdivided into 2×4 subzones. The character is separated into left and right parts, each of which consists of four horizontal sections. Hence, there are a total of eight sections labeled $S_h^1, S_h^2, ..., S_h^8$ in the character image input. Strip S_h^i consists of several lines. Suppose k lines of S_h^i, $\{\lambda_h^i \mid i = 1, 2, ..., k\}$, may touch the strokes of the character. This definition can be easily observed in Figure 2.53 demonstrating extraction of HPBA.

The more formal mathematical definition as presented in Tang [170] follows: Let $\mid \lambda_h^i \mid$ be the distance between the outermost stroke edge and the character image frame along line λ_h^i and $H_h^i \times V_h^i$ be the subarea of the ith horizontal section S_h^i. The horizontal peripheral background area in the ith horizontal section S_h^i is the quotient of the sum of $\mid \lambda_h^i \mid$'s in the ith horizontal section

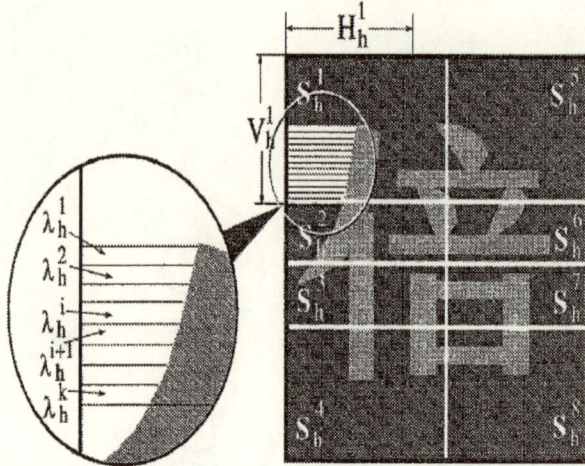

Figure 2.53: Feature extraction using HPBA and HPLD [170].

S_h^i divided by the subarea of the ith horizontal section S_h^i. The HPBA of the ith horizontal section S_h^i, denoted by $\aleph_h^i$ can be represented by the following formula:

$$\aleph_h^i = \left\{ \sum_{i=1}^{k} \mid \lambda_h^i \lambda \right\} / (H_h^i \times V_h^i)$$

VPBA is found in a very similar manner. First the character image is divided into 4×2 subframes. The character is separated into up and down parts, each of which consists of four vertical sections. The VPBA of the ith vertical section S_v^i, denoted by $\aleph_v^i$ can be represented by the following formula:

$$\aleph_v^i = \left\{ \sum_{i=1}^{k} \mid \lambda_v^i \lambda \right\} / (H_v^i \times V_v^i)$$

Alternative definitions of the Character Profile feature can be encountered in [184, 45, 94], but they are not sufficiently different from above to be granted detailed description.

2.5.5   Graph Description

Definitely a structural feature, *Graph Description* (GD) utilizes well developed mathematical graph theory to recognize different patterns. The first step is to extract the information about nodes and edges from the pattern, along with the description of the relationship between them. Theoretically any pattern can be described in terms of a graph with a certain number of interconnected nodes. Figure 2.54 shows graphs extracted by hand from letters 'K' and 'X'.

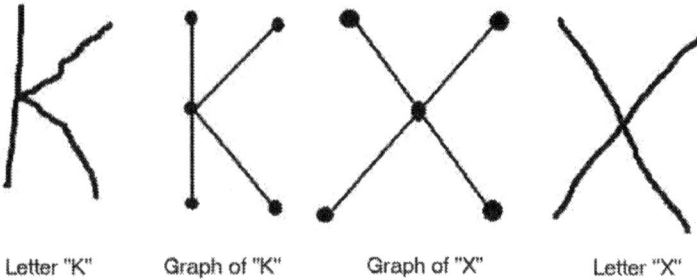

Letter "K"   Graph of "K"   Graph of "X"   Letter "X"

Figure 2.54: Demonstration of graph representations of letters 'K' and 'X'. It is clearly seen how different characters can have same graph morphology.

The main difficulty in applying this approach is to accurately extract the necessary information from the original image. Different line or circle detection algorithms can be utilized alongside with feature point detection procedures. After the graph description of an unknown pattern is extracted, it can be compared to the database of known graph templates. The type of the closest match is most likely the type of the pattern being investigated.

It is also seen from Figure 2.54 that sometimes different characters have morphologically equivalent graphs with exactly the same number of nodes and edges related in precisely the same way. This presents an additional difficulty with this approach, which can be solved by relying on additional information about the pattern. Overall, variations on the GD theme are very common with the character recognition researchers [9, 24, 25, 185], which make it a worthwhile to describe high-level feature.

2.5.6 Crossings Method

One of the oldest and most primitive methods, Crossing method is sometimes referred to as *Sonde* method in literature. While Sonde and crossing methods are very similar, a small but important difference exists, which will become apparent from the following descriptions.

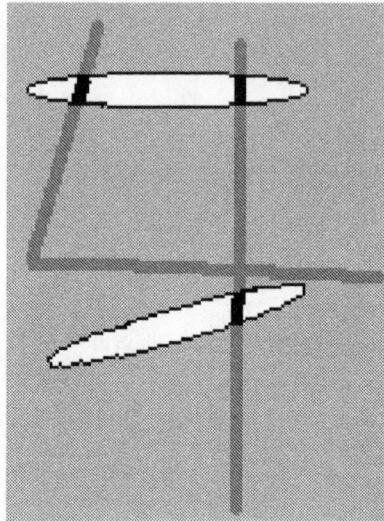

Figure 2.55: Method of stroke analysis via slits [161].

Slit Method

In its most primitive stages the method of crossings was identified with an observer looking at the pattern through the number of slits. The number of observed black regions for each slit is the value recorded as the feature being extracted. An example of slit analysis approach is shown in Figure 2.55, where two slits are used on digit '4' with upper slit showing two black regions and bottom slit containing just one black region [161].

Crossing Method

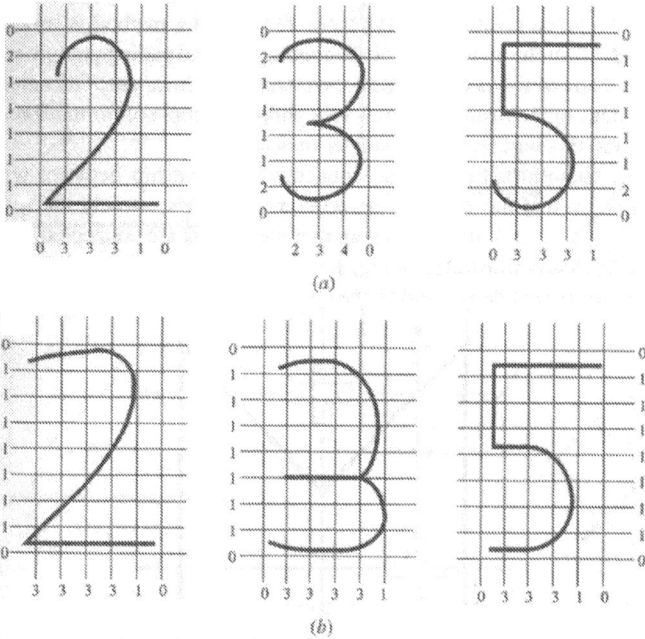

Figure 2.56: Crossing method. (a) '2' and '5' images can't be distinguished when only the vertical detecting lines are used; (b) '2', '3', and '5' images cannot be distinguished by the horizontal detecting lines [127].

A generalized version of slit method is shown in Figure 2.56. Relatively well known as Crossing method, it is close relative of Projection Histogram method (see section 2.3.1). As shown, the detecting lines are arranged parallel to the x-axis and the y-axis of the frame. The number of intersections with the detecting lines for a given input pattern is counted. In panel (a), if only the detecting lines parallel to the y-axis are counted, then '2' and '5' are not distinguishable, but this can be fixed by utilizing x-axis parallel detecting lines. In panel (b), some examples are shown where the input characters '2', '3', and '5' cannot be distinguished. This method is not affected by the position displacement of characters [127].

The crossing method is not invariant with respect to size of the input pattern. Contracting the count list is such a way that runs of the same count are neglected can counteract this. For example, $[0, 2, 2, 2, 3, 3, 3, 0]$ becomes $[0, 2, 3, 0]$. A side effect of this contraction is some loss of the information, particularly of relative length, such as no distinction is observed between '-' and '—' symbols.

Sonde Method

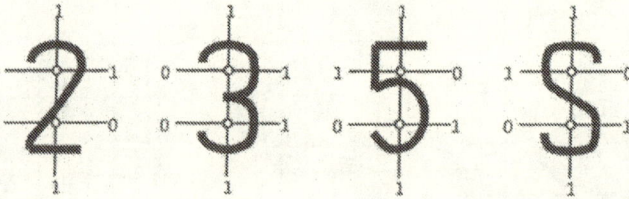

Figure 2.57: Sonde method. Extracted feature vectors shown under their respective patterns. Digit zero means not crossing and one denotes stroke crossing [127].

Sonde method is an adaptation of crossing method to the task of digit recognition. Crossing method due to its simplicity can be made slightly more powerful by observing that most digits (namely 2, 3, 5, 6, 8, 9) are written around two basic points shown as little circles at slit crossings in Figure 2.57. As a result each slit can be subdivided into two halves divided at such basic points with independent stroke crossing counts for each subslit. Figure 2.57 demonstrates just such an approach. If the input pattern crosses the bars, then '1' is counted, and otherwise '0' is recorded. This counts are shown as feature vectors under each one of the example characters '2', '3', '5', 'S'. An observant reader will notice that in this example the bar spanned between two focal points is neglected because this bar cannot effectively distinguish among the numerals '2', '3', and '5', while it is effective in discriminating them from digit '0', which is not part of this example [127].

This feature extraction methodology is only acceptable on very limited in its diversity patterns, such as digits. A perfect example of this, is panel (d) in Figure 2.57, which shows that a letter 'S' has the same feature vector as digit '5' after processing with Sonde method [127].

Both Sonde and Crossing methods are very simple approaches and as a result the loss of information content is very significant. Despite its obvious limitation, this feature extraction approach can be used if the number of categories of characters is limited and especially, if the character shapes are predefined as in the machine printed fonts [161].

The above-described methodology extracts local features of character strokes by looking from a window that is a very thin rectangle. If a stroke lies perpendicular to the window, then the local information about it will be extracted. Even if the stroke shifts in one of the two directions parallel to the stroke, the window can catch the stroke in the same way as before. For a given position displacement, the crossing method is invariant if the sequence of '0' in the count list in its beginning part and ending part are contracted. As a result, the shape of the distribution of the count list is invariant. The contraction of zeros at both sides of the distribution is a very simplistic example of normalization of feature space [127].

2.6   Transform Based Approaches

2.6.1   The Fourier Transform

Fourier Transform (FT) is a very popular tool for signal processing. It is a way to characterize the outer boundary of the character. It is reversible, meaning the original image is reconstructable, often from just a few coefficients. Also, Fourier feature can be made invariant to position, size and orientation of the pattern with some additional processing.

Two-dimensional version of Fourier transform can be directly applied to the image and the resulting coefficients can be used as features. Alternatively, a one-dimensional function of the image can be extracted and used instead of a 2D representation of the original pattern. Fourier processing in this case would be done on the 1D signal. In practice, the Fourier coefficients are computed for the contours of the pattern from some starting point to the current point. The lower coefficients describe the coarsest details of the pattern with the higher coefficients providing additional details.

Figure 2.58 demonstrates contours of the character 'A' reconstructed with an increasing number of Elliptic Fourier descriptors, a particular subtype of Fourier descriptor family

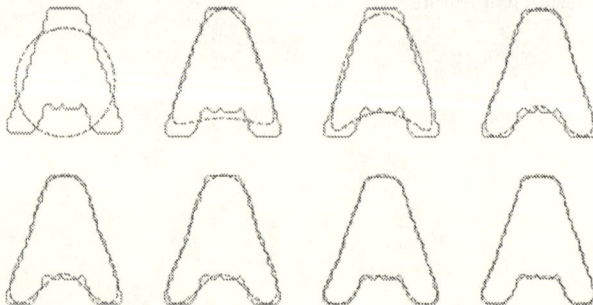

Figure 2.58: Contour of the character 'A' reconstructed with an increasing number of Elliptic Fourier descriptors. [119].

Fourier transforms are mathematically defined by [14, 119]:

$$f(x) = a_0 + \sum_{k=1}^{+\infty} (a_k \cos kx + b_k \sin kx) \tag{2.13}$$

where:

$$a_0 = 1/2\pi \int_0^{2\pi} f(x)dx \tag{2.14}$$

$$a_k = 1/2\pi \int_0^{2\pi} f(x)\cos(kx)dx \tag{2.15}$$

$$b_k = 1/2\pi \int_0^{2\pi} f(x)\sin(kx)dx \tag{2.16}$$

with a particular coefficient given by:

$$f_n(x) = a_0 + \sum_{k=1}^{n} (a_k \cos kx + b_k \sin kx)$$

Figure 2.59 shows 30 Fourier descriptors extracted from digits '2' and '6' [80].

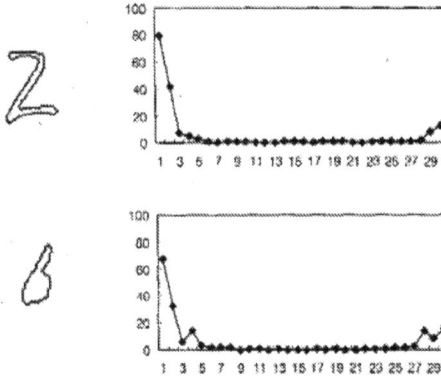

Figure 2.59: 30 Fourier descriptors extracted from digits '2' and '6' [80].

Fourier Transform is just one type of a transform used as a feature extraction method; multiple other transform based feature extraction methodologies exist:

- Zahn and Roskies Fourier Invariants [119]

- Elliptic Fourier Descriptors [180]

- Granlund's Elliptic Fourier Descriptors [119]

- Kuhl and Giardina's Elliptic Fourier Descriptors [185]

- Lin and Hwang's Elliptic Fourier Descriptors [42]

- Sinusoidal Kernel Transform [119]

- Discrete Cosine and Sine Transforms [119]

- Slang Transform [185]

- Walsh Hadamard Transform [119]

- Haar Transform [26]

- Hartley Transform [119]

- Polar and Log-Polar Transform [119]

- Karhunen Loeve Transform [59, 99, 197]

- Cubic Spline Approximation [185]

- Orthonormal-Shell-Fourier Descriptor [18, 19]

- Wavelet Transform [1, 35, 34, 72, 76, 82, 129, 157, 158]

- Hexagonal and Rectangular Wavelets [95]

- Biorthogonal Wavelets [27]

- Fourier Wavelet Descriptor [26]

- Wavelet Pocket Transform [155]

- Multiwavelet Transform [27]

Descriptions and some comparisons of different transform based approaches can also be found in [15, 33, 39, 58, 110, 116, 117, 118, 122, 207].

The share magnitude of different transforms indicates importance of this approach to pattern recognition in general and character recognition in particular. The approaches listed above have multiple practical implementations such as in a case of FT, which can be calculated as: Continuous, Discreet or Fast FT, with the last one being the most popular choice for obvious reason [158]. Different transforms also have different invariant properties and so a particular type of transform can be chosen based on the predominance of particular diversity type in the pattern pool [16]. Alternatively, good invariance properties of different transforms can be combined by creating features, which are based on a number of different transforms at the same time.

Quality of a transform as a feature extraction approach can be estimated based on its ability to reconstruct the original pattern, using as few coefficients as possible to approach a certain level of restoration accuracy. Figures 2.60, 2.61, 2.62, 2.63 and 2.64 show reconstruction ability of Elliptic Fourier Descriptors, Zahn and Ruskies' FT, and finally Granlund's FT.

Figure 2.60: Character '4' reconstructed by elliptic Fourier descriptors of orders up to: 1, 2, ..., 10, 15, 20, 30, 40, 50, 100 [185].

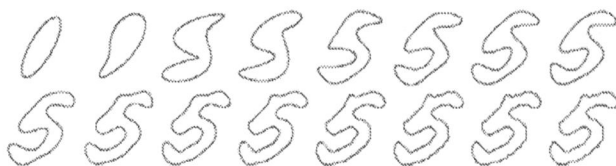

Figure 2.61: Character '5' reconstructed by elliptic Fourier descriptors of orders up to: 1, 2, ..., 10, 15, 20, 30, 40, 50, 100 [185].

Figure 2.62: Character 'S' reconstructed using the Zahn and Ruskies' Fourier transform with the number of coefficients equal to 5, 13, 25 and 65 [90].

Figure 2.63: Character 'S' reconstructed using the Granlund Fourier transform with the number of coefficients equal to 5, 13, 25 and 65 [90].

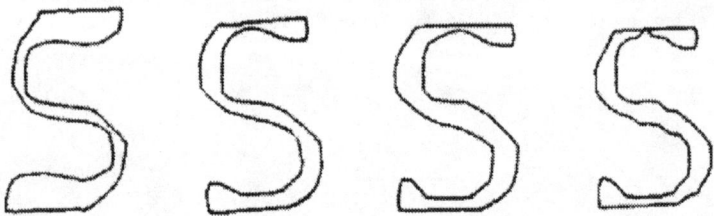

Figure 2.64: Character 'S' reconstructed using Zehn and Ruskies' FT modified by Krzyzak at al. Number of coefficients equal to 5, 13, 25 and 65 [90].

2.6.2   Gabor Filter

Gabor functions (GF) can be used to model cells in the visual cortex of mammals, and are capable of detecting strokes of particular orientation even of short length [74]. GF are a product of Gaussian and sinusoidal functions developed originally by Gabor, initially as signal carriers in communications [191]. An important property of GF is that they can achieve a joint optimal resolution with respect to both the spatial and spatial-frequency domains [73].

GF have been applied in computer vision, texture analysis, fingerprint recognition, face recognition and more recently in numerous character recognition applications [37, 56, 60, 61, 73, 189, 190, 202]. It is particularly useful in the Chinese and Japanese character recognition where it is capable of detecting strokes at 0°, 45°, 90° and 135° or any other desired orientation [195].

2D Gabor Filter is described by the impulse response [70]:

$$h(x,y) = g(x\cos\theta + y\sin\theta, -x\sin\theta + y\cos\theta)e^{j\lambda(x\cos\theta + y\sin\theta)}$$

where $g(x,y)$ is Gaussian given by;

$$g(x,y) = \frac{1}{\sqrt{2\pi\sigma_x\sigma_y}}e^{\frac{-((x/\sigma_x)^2 + (y/\sigma_y)^2)}{2}}$$

λ is the wavelength of Gabor filter and θ is the orientation angle of Gabor filter. σ_x, σ_y are the standard deviation of Gaussian along the x-direction and y-direction. The application of Gabor filter $h(x,y)$ to an image $I(x,y)$ results in the convolution sum:

$$S(x,y,\theta) = \sum_{x_1=x-\frac{M}{2}}^{x+\frac{M}{2}} \sum_{y_1=y-\frac{N}{2}}^{y+\frac{N}{2}} I(x_1,y_1)e^{\frac{-(x_1-x)^2-(y_1-y)^2}{2\sigma^2}}e^{j\lambda(\cos\theta(x-x_1)+\sin\theta(y_1-y))}$$

where M and N are dimensions of the Gabor filter.

In order to decrease the size of the feature vector, strokes in only a selected number of orientations should be detected. As a result, we need to be able to find optimal filter frequencies to be used by GF. Kyrki et al. [92] proposed a method for finding such filter frequencies. The strategy used is based on the possibility of using higher-level knowledge to determine the number of required orientations. If we take the smallest meaningful angle in the pattern to be α and let n represent the number of different orientations, we have:

$$\alpha = \frac{\pi}{n}$$

if d denotes the smallest distance, which can be measured in the image, the following relationship can be determined:

$$\sin \frac{\alpha}{2} = \frac{d}{2r}$$

where r is the radius of a circular area being inspected. We can find r as follows:

$$r = \frac{d}{2 \sin \frac{\alpha}{2}}$$

We conclude that the spatial radius of the GF must be at least r, as it is impossible to detect orientation changes with smaller spatial radius.

Figure 2.65 demonstrates an original character image being decomposed into four direction features according to the four basic directions. Darker color represents high directional feature [164]. Figure 2.66 shows orientation maps produced by Gabor filters for letters 'A', 'L', 'I' and 'o' with $r = .1$ and $r = 1.1$. It is easy to note that character 'o' which has uniform distribution of edge orientations produces an almost perfectly even distribution of edge frequencies [179]. Such orientation maps can serve as feature vectors, each uniquely representing a particular character.

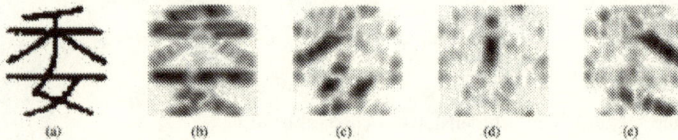

Figure 2.65: The results of using the Gabor filtering process: (a) an original image; (b)horizontal feature image; (c) right-diagonal feature image; (d) vertical feature image; (e) left-diagonal feature image [164].

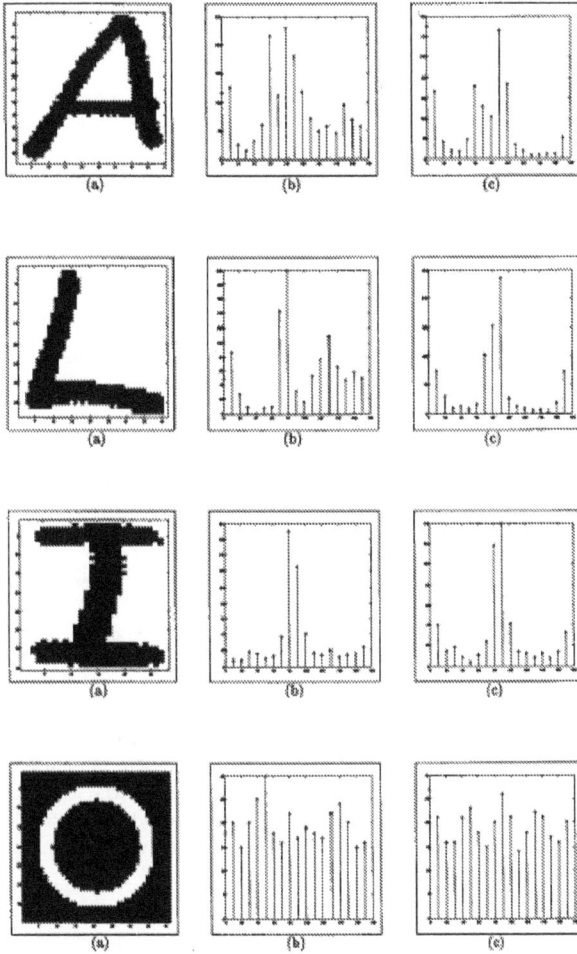

Figure 2.66: Orientation maps produced by Gabor filters for letters 'A', 'L', 'I' and 'o'. (b) $r = .1$; (c) $r = 1.1$[179].

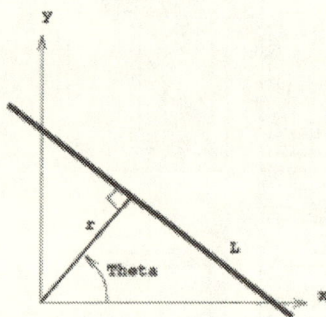

Figure 2.67: Hough trans-
form of a line [79].

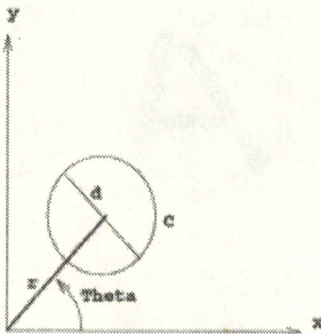

Figure 2.68: Hough trans-
form of a circle [79].

2.6.3 Hough Transform

The Hough Transform (HT) has been developed by Paul Hough in 1962 and
patented by IBM. Originally designed for detection of straight lines, it has
been later modified to include ability to detect curves, circles and ellipses.
Hough transform currently is a standard tool in the domain of computer
vision because it is particularly robust to missing and contaminated data.
This feature extraction technique requires that the image is presented in its
thinned/skeletonized form, since the thick strokes will result in many not
collinear lines detected for each stroke segment [119].

In the simplest case, HT of a line, the transform occurs from the (x, y)
space of the original image to the (r, θ) space. Figure 2.67 demonstrates the
relationship between the detected line and the r and θ variables. The origin
of the (x, y) space is the center of the image with individual pixels being
single units for both axes [79]. A line in the original image space (x, y) can
be defined by the equation:

$$x \cos \theta + y \sin \theta = r \qquad (2.17)$$

The parameter space can be subdivided into a number of bins, called
accumulators. Each such bin corresponds to a range of values of r and θ.

Figure 2.69: Hough trans-
form of a line on pattern 'p'
[79].

Figure 2.70: Generalized
Hough transform of circle
on pattern 'P' [79].

For each foreground pixel, all values of r are computed for all possible values of θ, and accumulators corresponding to all (r, θ) satisfying equation 2.17 get incremented by one. In case of a gray scale image, increment amount is taken to be equal to the intensity value of the pixel in the original image. A threshold can later be used to choose which bins have accumulated sufficient evidence for presence of a line. Length of the detected lines is directly related to the value of the used threshold and is at least as big [119]. The circles can be detected in a very similar way, the formula becomes:

$$(x - r \cos \theta)^2 + (y - r \sin \theta)^2 = (d/2)^2 \qquad (2.18)$$

and this time a three dimensional parameter space is used, namely: (r, θ, d) [120]. Figure 2.68 demonstrates the Hough transform for circles. A Hough transform of a preprocessed image of a machine-printed P is shown in Figure 2.69. The horizontal axes is the θ values and they range from 0° to 360°. The vertical axis is the r value and it ranges from 0 to 40 pixels. The grid lines are spaced in increments of 14.4 degrees in the horizontal and 2 pixels in the vertical direction. The image being transformed is shown on the left. The single long straight line in the 'P' is transformed into the bright spot at $(r = 12, \theta = 180^\circ)$. In Figure 2.70, a circle location extracted from the character 'P' using Hough transform is shown [79].

Hough transform is subject to the following properties:

1. In case of translation by a vector $V(x_V, y_V)$:

111

$r' = (x + x_V) \cos\theta + (y + y_V) \sin\theta =$
$x \cos\theta + y \sin\theta + x_V \cos\theta + y_V \sin\theta =$
$r + K(\theta)$, where $K(\theta) = x_V \cos\theta + y_V \sin\theta$. The row $a'[\theta]$ will be translated by $K(\theta)$.

2. Under dilation or contraction: the existing strokes will be longer or shorter, respectively. This results in $a'[r, \theta] > a[r, \theta]$ or $a'[r, \theta] < a[r, \theta]$ in case of contraction.

3. Under rotation by angle α:
$r' = (x \cos\alpha + y \sin\alpha) \cos\theta + (x \sin\alpha - y \cos\alpha) \sin\theta =$
$x \cos(\alpha - \theta) + \sin(\alpha - \theta)$
which results in $a'[r, \theta] = a[r, \alpha - \theta]$ and shift of columns $a'[r]$ by $\alpha - \theta$.

where a is the parameter space of the original image, and a' is the parameter space of the transformed image [119].

Some researches have attempted to utilize Hough transform as a feature extraction method for character recognition, using it for identification of Hebrew, Bengali, and Latin characters [79, 167, 149], while others applied it in an image retrieval application [120, 17].

Kushnier et al. [91] used Hough transform space to extract features necessary for classification of a subgroup of Hebrew characters. Hebrew language characters are particularly suitable for this type of treatment due to the fact that almost all of them are made up of a small number of simple strokes.

After thresholding out the bins with low cell count, the coordinates (r, θ) of the remaining cells were used as an extracted feature [91]. Since, the dimensionality of the feature vectors computed as stated above is variable, only first K cells (sorted by magnitude) were used in the final feature vectors. Simple feature template matching was used in order to appropriately classify characters and overall system performance was reported as being in high eighties [91].

Feature Maps

While recognizing handwritten Latin characters, Pinales at al. [149] used Hough space in order to extract the directional information about the original image. This information was stored in several feature maps having the same size as the character image. Feature map $M_k(x,y)$ is defined to be:

$$M_k(x,y) = \frac{h(x\cos\theta_k + y\sin\theta_k, \theta_k)}{\sum_\theta h(x\cos\theta + y\sin\theta, \theta)} I(x,y) \qquad (2.19)$$

where $\theta_k = \frac{\pi k}{N_\theta}, k = 0, ..., N_\theta - 1, x = 0, ..., X - 1$ and $y = 0, ..., Y - 1$, and $h(r,\theta)$ is the Hough transform of the original image, $I(x,y)$. The feature maps still contain all the information about the original image, as can be verified by checking that $I(x,y) = \sum_k M_k(x,y)$.

As the next step, Pinales at al. [149] extracted a set of local features from the information rich feature maps. For each zone they tried to detect the stroke orientations. In order to do that, they divided each feature map into a set of N_s parallel rectangular slices $\{R_i, t\}$ oriented at a given angle θ_t and at a distance r_i from the center of the image. Then, for each slice $\{R_i, t\}$ they computed local features by:

$$F_i * N_d * N_\theta + t * N_\theta + k = \frac{\sum_{x,y \in R_{i,t}} M_k(x,y)}{\sum_{j=0}^{N_\theta - 1} \sum_{x,y \in R_{i,t}} M_j(x,y)} \qquad (2.20)$$

where $i = 0, 1, ..., N_s - 1, t = 0, 1, ..., N_d - 1, k = 0, 1, ..., N_\theta - 1, N_s$ is the number of parallel slices, N_d is the number of slice orientations and N_d is the number of feature maps [149].

Modified Hough Transform

A slight modification to the process of feature extraction by Hough transform was suggested by Singh et al. [160]. They noticed that HT is subject to a significant limitation, namely, the value computed by accumulator cells is not necessarily the size of the single continuous stroke in the original pattern that is located along this line. This occurs as a result of HT only considering individual points. The total value in the accumulator cell is the sum of those points along an infinitely long line through the original pattern, which is not necessarily a continuous line. As a result, Hough transform is very likely to concentrate on short line segments, which just happen to be located on the same line in terms of (r, θ).

In order to verify the presence of a genuine continuous line, Singh et al.

[160] propose looking at the original image and noting which points actually lie on the infinite line and whether they do in fact form a continuous stroke. As line is being traced from there, it enters the image to where it exits; we are likely to encounter some gaps in the stroke. By scanning over empty space, we can see if the line continuous after a certain distance has been passed along the stroke's path. In addition, keeping the count of encountered pixels would allow us to determine the actual length of the stroke. As part of this process, gaps and noise in the image can be eliminated if not already taken care of in the preprocessing stage [160].

Fuzzy Hough Transform

Sural et al. [167] used a modified Hough transform in order to recognize Bengali characters. Hough transform was employed as a way of getting structural information about the patterns. See Section 2.5.1 to learn more about structural features. Since, usually thresholding is applied to accumulator cells, some of the important information may be lost in the process. In order to solve this problem, researchers proposed a fuzzy approach, based on fuzzy sets, for extracting information from Hough space accumulator cells. Called *Fuzzy Set Membership Functions* (FSMF), they are listed in Figure 2.72 for θ values in first quadrant. Similar membership functions are defined for θ values in the other quadrants as well [169].

The fuzzy sets presented in Figure 2.72 serve the following purpose: LL and SL extract length information of the different lines in the character pattern. HL, VL and TL represent their skew, while NT, NB, NVC, NR, NL and NHC provide spatial distribution of these lines. Using those FSMF, the characteristics of the original pattern can be described. The following properties can be attributed to above-mentioned FSMF:

1. $\mu_A(x) \in [0, 1]$, where A is a fuzzy set from Figure 2.72

2. The height of each fuzzy set, $h(A) = 1$ and so each such set is normal.

3. The core of the fuzzy sets TL, NT, NB, NVC, NR, NL, NHC represents crisp features. The core of the fuzzy sets HL and VL stand for strictly horizontal or vertical lines. The core of LL is a diagonal line.

4. Fuzzy sets LL and SL denote straight lines with all possible lengths in the pattern [167].

114

Based on FSMF shown in Figure 2.72, Sural at al. [167] synthesized additional fuzzy sets to represent each line in an original character pattern as a combination of its length, orientation and positioning. The actual membership values for those new fuzzy sets are determined using intersections of the basic fuzzy sets, also known as *t-norms*. A fuzzy intersection or a t-norm i is a binary operation on the unit interval that satisfies the following properties for any $p, q, r, \in [0, 1]$

1. $i(p, l) = p$

2. $q \leq r \Rightarrow i(p, q) \leq i(p, r)$

3. $i(p, q) = i(q, p)$

4. $i(p, i(q, r)) = i(i(p, q), r)$

5. $i(p, q) = min(p, q)$, standard intersection used by Sural at al.

where p, q, r stand for membership values in arbitrary fuzzy sets. T-norm based synthesized fuzzy set definitions utilized by Sural are summarized in Figure 2.74, which includes both definitions and the notation used [168].

Amongst the synthesized fuzzy sets, the following definitions are proposed:

- *Long Slant Line near the Left (LSL)* $\equiv i(i(TL, LL), NL)$

- *Short Slant Line near the Right (SSR)* $\equiv i(i(TL, SL), NR)$

- *Nearly Vertical Long Line near the Left (VLL)* $\equiv i(i(VL, LL), NL)$

- etc.

In the same way circle-based Hough transform fuzzy sets are defined, namely, *Small Circle* (SC), *Dense Sircle* (DS), *Near Top* (NP), *Near Centre* (NC), etc., as well as synthesized ones: *Small Dense Circle near the Top* (SDT), *Large Dense Circle near the Center* (LDC), etc. Figure 2.71 demonstrates above-mentioned fuzzy sets used for circle detection in the work under consideration [168].

In terms of the values obtained from synthesized fuzzy sets, any nonzero output implies the existence of the corresponding feature in the original pattern. As a result, Sural et al. [167] chose the height of each such synthesized fuzzy set to define a feature element. They took a compilation of such feature elements as an assembled feature vector for a particular character. Some of the fuzzy feature element extracted from Bengali characters by Sural et al. can be seen in Figure 2.73.

In its essence, Fuzzy Hough transform is not really a feature, rather it is an extremely powerful methodology for extracting high level features from the image. As such is a very useful tool in particular to someone interested in identifying structural information in artificial patterns such as scanned characters. While the presents of even few noise pixels can result in so-called ghost lines being incorrectly detected by Hough transform, it is still accurate enough to allow high degree of recognition even for difficult alphabets such as Hebrew of Bengali.

Fuzzy Set	Membership Function		Notation
Large circle	$\left(\dfrac{c}{X/2}\right)$		LC
Small circle	2LC	if $c \le (X/4)$	SC
	2(1-LC)	if $c > (X/4)$	
Centre near right border	$\left(\dfrac{a}{Y}\right)$		CRB
Centre near left border	1-CRB		CLB
Centre near horizontal mid-point	2CRB	if $a < (Y/2)$	CHM
	2(1-CRB)	otherwise	
Centre near top border	$\left(\dfrac{b}{X}\right)$		CTB
Centre near bottom border	1-CTB		CBB
Centre near vertical mid-point	2CTB	if $b < (X/2)$	CVM
	2(1-CTB)	otherwise	
Centre near mid-point	(2CHM)CVM		CMP
Dense circle	$\left(\dfrac{cosnt}{2\pi c}\right)$		DC
Sparse circle	2DC	if Count $\le \pi c$	PC
	2(1-DC)	Otherwise	

Figure 2.71: Fuzzy set membership functions defined on Hough transform accumulator cells for circle detection from a pattern of height X and width Y [168].

116

Fuzzy Set	Membership Function	Notation
Long line	$\left(\dfrac{count}{\sqrt{X^2+Y^2}}\right)$	LL
Short line	$2LL$ if count $\leq \dfrac{\sqrt{X^2+Y^2}}{2}$ $2(1-LL)$ if count $> \dfrac{\sqrt{X^2+Y^2}}{2}$	SL
Nearly horizontal line	$\left(\dfrac{\theta}{90.0}\right)$	HL
Nearly vertical line	$1-HL$	VL
Slant line	$2HL$ if $\theta \leq 45.0$ $2(1-HL)$ if $\theta > 45.0$	TL
Line near top border	$\left(\dfrac{\rho}{X}\right)$ if $HL > VL$ 0 otherwise	NT
Line near bottom border	$1-NT$ if $HL > VL$ 0 otherwise	NB
Line near vertical centre	$2NT$ if $(HL > VL$ and $\rho \leq \dfrac{X}{2})$ $2(1-NT)$ if $(HL > VL$ and $\rho > \dfrac{X}{2})$ 0 otherwise	NVC
Line near right border	$\left(\dfrac{\rho}{Y}\right)$ if $VL > HL$ 0 otherwise	NR
Line near left border	$1-NR$ if $VL > HL$ 0 otherwise	NL
Line near horizontal centre	$2NR$ if $(VL > HL$ and $\rho \leq \dfrac{Y}{2})$ $2(1-NR)$ if $(VL > HL$ and $\rho > \dfrac{Y}{2})$ 0 otherwise	NHC

Figure 2.72: Membership functions of fuzzy sets defined on Hough transform accumulator cells. X and Y denote the height and width of each character pattern [167].

117

Character Pattern	Hough cell size ($\Delta\rho$, $\Delta\theta$) = (0.5.1°), (Δa, Δb, Δc) = (1,1,0.5)				
	Values of the feature elements				
	LSL	SSR	VLL	SDT	LDC
অ	0.32	0.81	0.19	0.89	0.31
উ	0.42	0.45	0.25	0.94	0.52
ঋ	0.63	0.83	0.21	0.43	0.13
ব	0.63	0.96	0.13	0.31	0.35
খ	0.25	0.33	0.12	0.20	0.27
চ	0.36	0.14	0.88	0.46	0.14
ধ	0.29	0.78	0.25	0.55	0.35
ঙ	0.28	0.32	0.27	0.91	0.62

Figure 2.73: Some of the fuzzy features extracted by Hough transform from eight scanned Bengali characters [167].

Synthesized Fuzzy Set	Definition (i = t-norm)	Notation
Long slant line	t(TL,LL)	LSL
Short slant line	t(TL,SL)	SSL
Nearly horizontal short line near vertical centre	t(HL,SL,NVC)	HSVC
Nearly vertical long line near left border	t(VL,LL,NL)	VLL
Nearly vertical long line near right border	t(VL,LL,NR)	VLR
Nearly horizontal long line near top border	t(HL,LL,NT)	HLT
Nearly horizontal long line near bottom border	t(HL,LL,NB)	HLB
Nearly vertical long line near horizontal centre	t(VL,LL,NHC)	VLHC
Nearly vertical short line near horizontal centre	t(VL,SL,NHC)	VSHC
Large dense circle with centre near mid-point	t(LC,DC,CMP)	LDM
Large sparse circle with centre near mid-point	t(LC,PC,CMP)	LPM
Large sparse circle with centre near bottom border on horizontal mid-point	t(LC,PC,CBB,CHM)	LPBM
Small sparse circle with centre near left border on vertical mid-point	t(SC,PC,CLB,CVM)	SPLM
Small dense circle with centre near top border on horizontal mid-point	t(SC,DC,CTB,CHM)	SDTM
Small sparse circle with centre near top left border	t(SC,PC,CTB,CLB)	SPTL
Small sparse circle with centre near top right border	t(SC,PC,CTB,CRB)	SPTR
Small sparse circle with centre near bottom border on horizontal mid-point	t(SC,PC,CBB,CHM)	SPBM
Small sparse circle with centre near mid-point	t(SC,PC,CMP)	SPM
Small dense circle with centre near mid-point	t(SC,DC,CMP)	SDM

Figure 2.74: Synthesized fuzzy set definitions using t-norms [168].

118

2.6.4   Chain Code

The Chain Code method is a popular end robust method for representing contours of different objects. The basic idea was introduced in 1961 by Freeman, and so it is sometimes referred to as *Freeman Coding* [119]. In this approach, an arbitrary curve is represented by a sequence of small vectors of unit length and a limited set of possible directions, thus termed the *Unit-Vector* method. Figure 2.75 shows two most popular types of chain coding, namely 4- and 8-dirrectional chain codes [123].

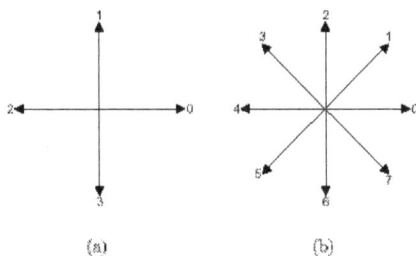

Figure 2.75: Chain code numbering schemes: (a) Directions for 4-directional chain code. (b) Directions for 8-direcional chain code [123].

Encoding is based on the fact that successive contour points are adjacent to each other. Depending on whether the 4-connected or the 8-connected grid is employed, the chain code is defined as the digits from 0 to 3 or 0 to 7. A chain can be coded by the absolute image address of one of its points followed by the relative position of the remaining points to their predecessors. In case of isolated character encoding, absolute position of the starting pixel is irrelevant and so can be omitted. On the other hand, the determination of the starting point is an important factor once it comes time to compare two chain coded patterns, since the same pattern can give very different feature vectors based on the selected starting point [194].

Figure 2.76 shows a contour shape encoded with the Chain Code method,

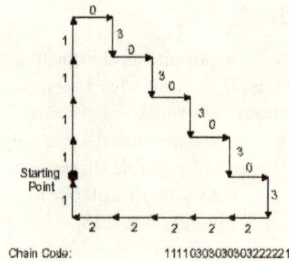

Figure 2.76: An example of the 4-directional chain code representation [123].

including the starting point which is shown, but not included in the extracted feature itself. In its pure form, Chain Code is not an ideal feature for character recognition, but its many modifications have been successfully used by multiple researchers (see following subsections). In its unchanged form, Chain Coding has been used in combination with other methodologies as a way to achieve stroke extraction, structure and shape description, noise reduction as well as line detection. Interested reader is directed to [24, 31, 43, 100, 114, 135, 194, 205] for detailed information.

Normalized Generalized Chain Code

Generalized Chain Code (GCC) is a special type of chain coding that uses as its bases multiple concentric coding rings. To improve efficiency, the number of ring sizes that can be used is limited, and they are usually determined in advance in order to assign unique binary codes to all the vector nodes. The actual coding ring size used at each coding step is determined based on the smoothness of the trace in such a way that a larger coding ring should encode a longer straight curve segment. Figure 2.77 shows the conventional $(1, 2, 3)$-GCC coding rings [111, 203].

Yuen in [203] proposes a new chain coding method for real-time recognition of on-line handwritten characters, he calls it Normalized Generalized Chain Code. The proposed GCC approach does not require and predetermined coding ring size since it includes all the possible coding rings. The

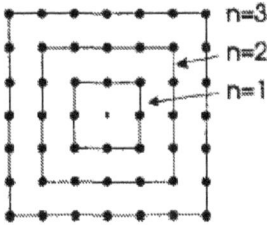

Figure 2.77: Conventional $(1, 2, 3)$-Generalized Chain Code coding rings [203].

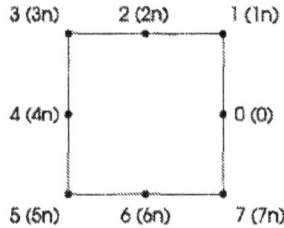

Figure 2.78: Normalized GCC 8-node ring [203].

proposed GCC code contains just two parameters. The first one is the specific coding ring order n. Each coding ring contains $M = 8n$ nodes, where $n = 1, 2, 3, ...$ The second parameter is the actual node number i, where $i = 0, 1, 2, ..., 8n - 1$ [203].

The NGCC code has a dynamic range of $0 \leq i/n < 8$, which has an affect of reducing the NGCC ring to having only eight primary nodes as shown in Figure 2.78, along with some eight unnormalized nodes shown in brackets. The NGCC coding is equivalent to the chain coding shown in right part of Figure 2.75 [203]. Since this feature was used solely in on-line character recognition, we will not go into further details as this survey concentrates on the off-line feature extraction methods and so NGCC is beyond its scope.

Chain Code Histogram

This method is a way of combining Chain Codes with the idea of image zoning (see Section 2.2.3) and Projection Histograms (see Section 2.3.1). Actually, the image zoning is completely optional as the whole pattern can be subjected to the same exact process. Basically in the process of generating this feature for some region of the input image, we generate the Chain Code representation of the object. Either four or eight different values make up the new representation depending on the Chain Coding method selected. For each zone of interest we compute the total number of occurrences of unit vectors of each type, which we represent as a regular histogram. Figure 2.79 demonstrates this process from the beginning to the end for the square like example shape [77].

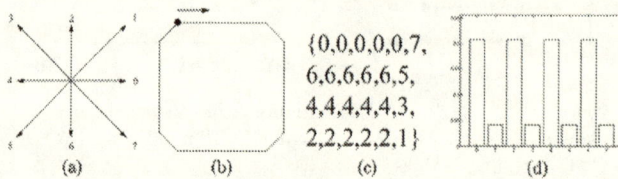

Figure 2.79: (a) The 8-directional Freeman chain code; (b) The contour of a sample shape, square; (c) Chain Code representation of a square; (d) The Chain Code Histogram of the square [77].

Chain Code Histogram is a discrete function

$$p(k) = n_k/n$$

where n_k is the number of chain code values k in a chain code, and n is the number of links in a chain code. The CCH shows the probabilities for different directions present in the contour. One of the advantages of the CCH is its independence of the choice of the starting point. However, the chain coding direction (clockwise or counterclockwise) should be same for all patterns. The CCH is a translation and scale invariant feature. It can be made invariant to rotation of 90° because the 90° rotations cause only a circular shift in the CCH. To achieve better rotation invariance the Normalized Chain Code Histogram was proposed by Iivarinen et al. [77]. Unlike CCH, it takes into account the lengths of the different directions. The NCCH is defined as

$$p_n(k) = (l_k n_k)/l$$

where n_k is the number of chain code values k in the chain code, l_k is the length of the direction k, and l is the length of the contour. For example, in case of 8-directional chain code, $l_k = 1$, $k = 0, 2, 4, 6$, and $l_k = \sqrt{2}$, $k =$

$1, 3, 5, 7$. The NCCH can be made invariant to discrete rotations of $(360/K)^o$, where K is the number of direction in the chain code. In theory by making K very large, rotation invariance can be achieved. In practice, discrete nature of the pattern causes some errors [77].

Overall, CCH method is mentioned by multiple researchers including Cao [23] and Laaksonen [94].

Chain Code Transform

In a manner similar to Hough Transform (HT) (see Section 2.6.3), Chain Code Transform (CCT) is another approach to transforming an image into the parameter space $r - \theta$. Proposed in 1985 by Cheung et al. [29] this method was aimed at retaining good properties of HT, while improving on the noise sensitivity problem, which is the main drawback of the Hough Transform methodology [119].

CCT is based on simple chain code encoding approach followed by one additional step, namely parameter transformation. After the character is thinned and chain-code tracing is performed using the 4-directional chain code, the information about the directions and positions of the strokes are extracted from the chain-coded character and recorded in the $r - \theta$ plane. Each pixel is considered as a single stroke segment with the direction θ given by its chain-coded label which is quantized into four directions [29]. The perpendicular distance r from the origin to the stroke segment is calculated from the coordinates (x, y) of the pixel according to the following equation:

$$r = \begin{cases} x & if\ c_i = 0 \\ \sqrt{2}/2(x - y) & if\ c_i = 1 \\ y & if\ c_i = 2 \\ \sqrt{2}/2(x + y) & if\ c_i = 3 \end{cases}$$

The parameter space is subdivided into rectangular cells with a contour set up in each cell. For each pixel of the pattern being examined, the contour of the cell at the corresponding (r, θ) coordinates are incremented. The algorithm is demonstrated in Figure 2.80 where a 45° stroke is shown in Figure 2.80 (a). The thinned stroke and its chain coded equivalent are given in

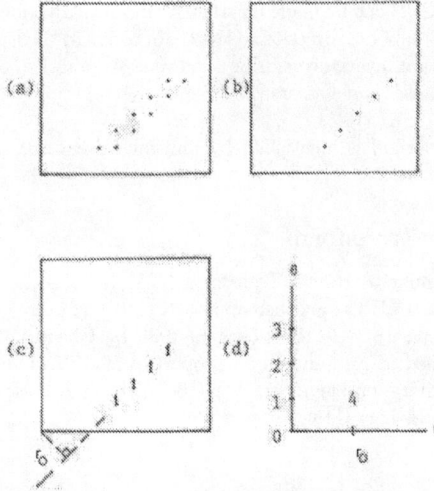

Figure 2.80: Example of Chain Code Transform: (a) A 45° stroke; (b) Same stroke after thinning; (c) Stroke labeled with chain-codes; (d) Transformed pattern [29].

Figures 2.80 (b) and 2.80 (c) respectively. The transformed pattern is given in Figure 2.80 (d), where the counter in the corresponding (r, θ) coordinate registers the number '4', which is equal to the length of the detected stroke [29].

Main advantage of CCT versus Hough Transform approach is its low sensibility to noise and high speed. In comparative tests, conducted by Cheung et al. [29] CCT also showed higher recognition levels when used on a set of complex Asian characters [29, 119].

Run Length Coding

Chain Coding is not the only approach to image compression. Another popular alternative, which made its way into the world of character features is the so-called *Run-Length* coding approach. While many variations exist, the main idea behind Run-Length Coding (RLC) is very simple and is demonstrated in Figure 2.81 [131]. Since, while describing any pattern, we are only interested in the information contained in the foreground, we can safely ignore background information. So, RLC is just shorthand for describing foreground information.

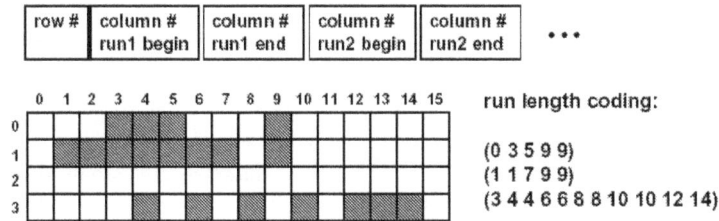

row #	column # run1 begin	column # run1 end	column # run2 begin	column # run2 end	⋯

run length coding:

(0 3 5 9 9)
(1 1 7 9 9)
(3 4 4 6 6 8 8 10 10 12 14)

Figure 2.81: Run Length coding example [131].

In order to fully describe the pattern, all we need is for every row of the image to specify the locations of the beginning and end points of each run of set-on pixels. The format for that type of encoding is shown at the top of Figure 2.81.

Typically RLC is used as the methodology in the stroke extraction approach, particularly as it pertains to Asian character recognition. Fan et al. [46] utilized Run-Length coding for stroke extraction from Chinese characters without using thinning preprocessing step. This is done in order to avoid distortions around junction area generated by typical thinning process. In order to capture the complete range of possible stroke directions, non-vertical and non-horizontal Run-Length descriptors are introduced, particularly at 45 and 135 degrees [46].

Run-Length Coding can also be used for simple handwriting compression as demonstrated by work of Yuen et al. Interested reader is directed to [204] for details, which are beyond the scope of this book.

Compensated Run Length Coding

In their work, Mori et al. [125, 126] utilize RLC for robust recognition of deformed or degraded Kanji characters. While the general idea of individual stroke extraction remains the same as with Fan et al. [46], they postulate that the degradation of the image comes from additive and subtractive noise. As the intensity of these types of noise increases, stroke run length becomes harder to extract. In order to resolve this, they go one step beyond and introduce a new approach they call *Compensated Run Length* (RLC), which can better extract the stroke directional information from characters corrupted by noise. RLC utilizes the complementary relationship between additive and subtractive noise in terms of black and white runs.

In the experiments described by Mori et al. [125, 126], CRL is not really an independent feature rather it is a methodology for extracting stroke information about Asian characters, which is later utilized as the feature based on which classification is performed. Stroke information by itself would be classified as the structural feature (see Section 2.5.1) in this book. As a result, no detailed description of the proposed by Mori et al. algorithm is presented here. An interested reader is guided to the original papers by Mori et al. [125, 126] for detailed information regarding implementation of CRL and evaluation of its performance.

2.7   Fractal Based Approaches

2.7.1   Fractal Encoding

Trees, coastlines, snowflakes and many other natural phenomena are believed to exhibit fractal properties, meaning they contain at different scales smaller copies of itself. Similar idea can be applied to the description of individual characters. Non-fractal images, such as characters, can be made self-similar by covering them with affine transformations of the original image.

The set of transformations becomes the descriptive feature in this case. The parameters used to describe affine transformations are the features used to characterize each character. Since we only want to recognize characters and not fully reconstruct them, a small number of transformations is sufficient. An algorithm for automated determination of complete affine-transformation covering is given in work of Baldoni [8].

Main advantage of this methodology is the fact that the number of features used for encoding the character is not dependent on the size of the image, but only on the complexity of the pattern being recognized. Figure 2.82 shows hand-constructed fractal encoding of digits '1','4' and '7'. Figure 2.83 shows how a printed character 'F' could be approximated with six affine-tranformation of itself. Finally, figure 2.84 shows a fractal encoding of digit '7' generated using algorithm developed by Baldoni at. el [8].

(a)   (b)   (c)

Figure 2.82: (a) Binarized digits '1','4' and '7'; (b) Digit covering with four self-affine transformations; (c) Digit fractal reconstruction [8].

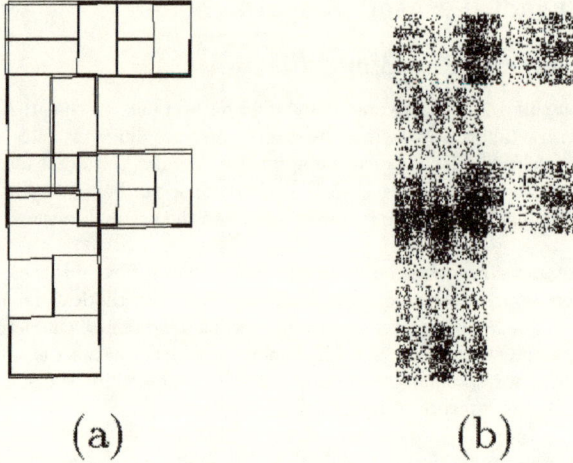

(a)   (b)

Figure 2.83: 'F' is covered with six contracted copies of itself, each bar is being covered with two contracted copies placed side by side [8].

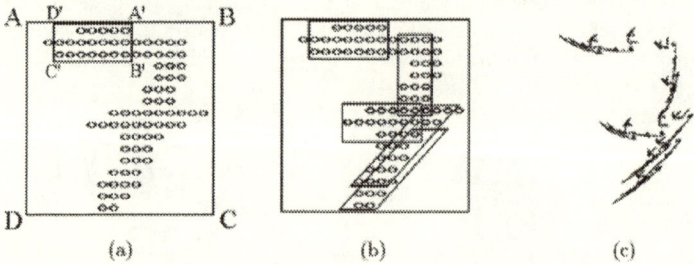

Figure 2.84: (a) Digit '7' inside the square box ABCD and application of first affince contraction resulting in A'B'C'D'; (b) Coverage using five contractions; (c) Fractal reconstruction [8].

2.7.2   Fractal Feature

The underlining idea of Fractal Feature (FF) is similar to that of Fractal Encoding, but in the latter case additional properties of the fractals are used as a feature. More specifically the idea of the fractal dimension is being explored by such researchers as Tang et al. [171, 172, 177, 178]. Fractal dimension contains information about geometric structure of the fractal, it determines how much 'space' it takes between arbitrary m and $m+1$ dimensional manifolds [174].

Multiple approaches to determining the fractal dimension exist, such as *Hausdorff* dimension, *Minkowski* dimension, *Divider* dimension and a very popular *Box Counting* dimension (BCD) [177].

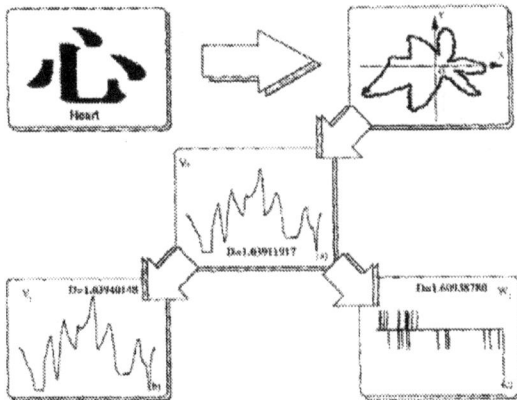

Figure 2.85: Diagram of feature extraction by Fractal Feature for the Chinese character "Heart" [174].

BCD is popular because it is easy to compute or to estimate. Let F be a non-empty and bounded subset of $\Re^n$, and $\xi = \{w_i : 1, 2, 3...\}$ be covers of the set F. $N_\delta(F)$ denotes the number of covers, such that

$$N_\delta(F) = |\xi : d_i \leq \delta|$$

The Box Counting Dimension can be defined by the following:

$$dim_B F = \lim_{\delta \to 0} \frac{\log_2 N_\delta(F)}{-\log_2 \delta}$$

In the feature extraction method proposed by Tang et al. [174] a complex multi-step process is involved. First, central projection of the 2D image is acquired. Next, a wavelet transformation of the 1D projection from step one is obtained. Finally, computation of the divider dimension for the wavelet pattern is performed. The last step is performed three consecutive times, which results in three feature vectors. Figures 2.85 and 2.86 show the computed Divider dimensions for different characters.

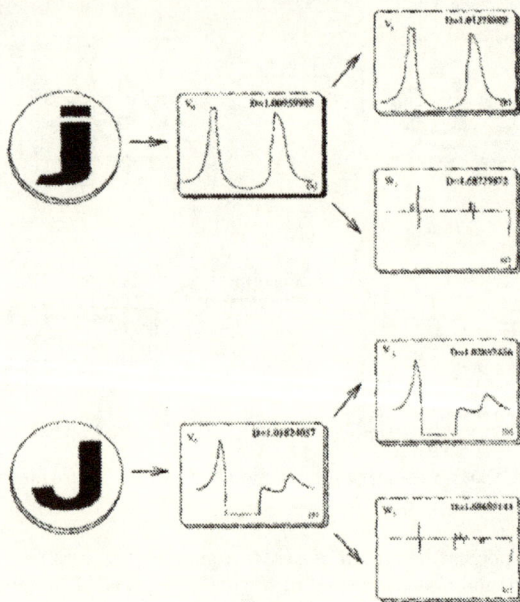

Figure 2.86: Diagram of feature extraction by Fractal Feature for the characters 'I' and 'J' [174].

2.8   Other Approaches

2.8.1   Characteristic Loci

One of the features, which processes the background of the image rather than the character itself is the so called *Characteristic Loci* feature. Suggested by Glucksman in 1967, this method has never been improved on, judging by the available literature, and now is almost completely obsolete [57, 119]. The major idea is that for every background pixel a 4-tuple is computed with each entry representing the number of times a ray omitted in one of the four directions (East, West, South, North) would intersect the actual pattern of interest. Figure 2.87 demonstrates a 4-tuple computed for a point inside some hypothetical character.

It is interesting to note that the way the idea was presented in the original paper involved a conscious observer standing on a particular pixel within the image making visual observations of the four directions, and reporting his findings. A number of such observers at different points in the image would communicate their findings in order to arrive at a common decision as to the nature of the character being observed [57].

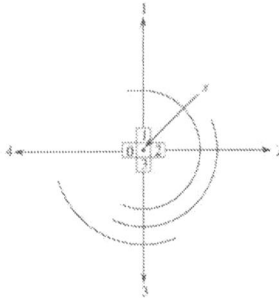

Figure 2.87: 4-tuple calculated for the hypothetical background pixel x [127].

131

Mathematically this feature can be defined as:

$$f_i = \frac{\#S_i}{\#(S_1 \cup S_2 \cup ... \cup S_N)} \qquad (2.21)$$

where $\#S$ is the cardinality of the set S. Individual sets are built based on the described above principal, namely, for each turned off pixel in the image a code is calculated. Pixels p_i and p_j, which share the same code C_i, get grouped together in a set S_i respectively. From this definition the main problem with this feature can be deduced, namely its high dimensionality. Based on the type of characters that are being recognized the number of possible codes can become extremely large [119]. For example if we take Asian characters, which are made up of between 4 and 40 strokes, we will end up with: $N = 40^4$, which is 2560000 potential codes. Clearly, this is not useful due to its high dimensionality.

Glucksman performed his experiments on the Roman alphabet. In that case he only had to deal with 256 possible codes, since maximum number of used strokes is limited to 4, $N = 4^4$. Unfortunately, back in 1960 computers were not as fast as they are today and so even that was too much to handle. As a result, Glucksman proposed a variety of methods in order to further reduce the number of possible codes. Since he worked with a relatively low in complexity character sets, he suggested only using three possible values, namely: 0 - meaning no intersection, 1 - one intersection and 2 - any other number of intersections. This results in 81 possible codes, still excessive by 1960's standards [127].

Glucksman suggested only considering background pixels, which are located inside the bounding box for the character. This removes all the codes, which contain mostly zeroes. The suggested bounding box can be seen in figure 2.88. Finally, Glucksman decided to combine all sets where exactly two corresponding digits are zero. This means that $c_i = [0, x_i, y_i, 0]$ and $c_j = [0, x_j, y_j, 0]$ can be grouped together in a generalized code $[0, 1, 1, 0]$, representing corner pixels for connected patterns. This process is demonstrated in figure 2.88. This left Glucksman to consider only fifty one different code combinations [119].

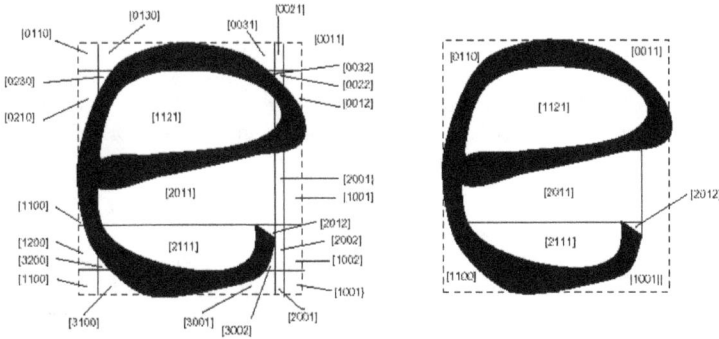

Figure 2.88: Left: full ternary code. Right: 4-tuples with three or four zeroes removed [119].

Depending on just how simple the character set in question is, one might consider reducing the coding scheme to its binary variation, where a 0 - means no intersections and a 1 - is for any number of intersections other than zero. This reduces the code dimensionality to just around 16 possible combinations, but unfortunately most useful information is lost as well. Characters with somewhat similar shape will not be as recognizable, for example 'e' and 'c' [119].

The fact that this feature is not currently being used can be explained by its extreme sensitivity to noise or defects in the image. Even a single incorrectly set pixel is capable of changing the resulting codes. Characteristic loci feature is also sensitive to shape variations making it perform less than acceptably on handwritten characters. No professional grade literature is available reporting experiments on Asian or Arabic characters using Characteristic Loci, which lets us conjecture that due to the "curse of dimensionality" as well as to above mentioned shortcoming. This feature is now mostly of historical interest and has no potential for future research.

2.8.2   N-Tuple

The N-tuple feature was originally proposed by Bledsoe [12] in December of 1959. So, it makes it one of the oldest known feature extraction methods used in character recognition, but despite its age it is still a valuable feature extraction technique as demonstrated by its ongoing use, see work of Anderson [3] for one of the latest examples.

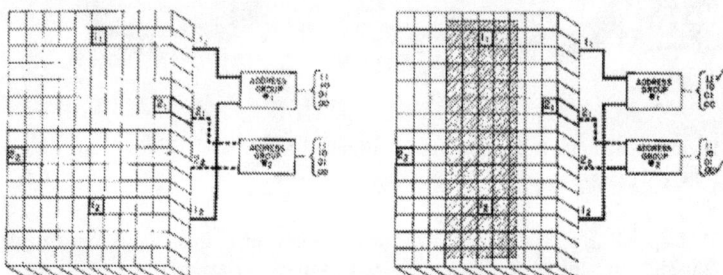

Figure 2.89: Left: locations of the two 2-tuples. Right: Same two 2-tuples learning letter 'I' and the resulting memory states [12].

The basic idea behind the method is to take sample measurements at different points in the image and see if a particular relationship holds. Assuming we are dealing with a binary image, for every sample point we get either a 1 or a 0 representing a set or a turned-off pixel respectively. Each such sampling gives us a 1-tuple, which does provide some useful information. Unfortunately due to the shifting in location of the character within the image, same exact sample point can result in complementary binary values being produced by the same character. This problem is the result of 1-tuple features, lacking information about relative states of other points within the image. This can be easily corrected by using $n > 1$, as the size for our n-tuple.

Figure 2.89 demonstrates an image being sampled with two 2-tuples. For each tuple four possible results can be produced: 00 or 01 or 10 or 11.

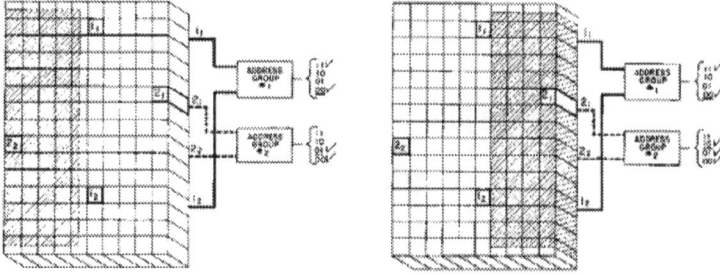

Figure 2.90: System learning letter 'I' in two different locations within the image [12].

Right subimage of figure 2.89 demonstrates the system learning letter 'I'. If character is shifted within the image, different memory states will arise as can be seen in figure 2.90, but some states are impossible to be generated by certain characters despite any amount of shifting. Bledsoe and Browning, [12], gave particular emphasis to this property of their method:

> ...the very shape of the character, such as the letter 'I' forbids certain states for certain pairs. The existence of these states lies at the heart of our method, for without them the logic would saturate...

A more formal, mathematical definition of the n-tuple method is presented in [119]. Input image is seen as string S, whose size is equal to the number of pixels in the input image. S is divided into N sub-strings S_i, which are referred to as n-tuples. If presented as binary numbers have a value between 0 and $2^n - 1$ and form an N-dimensional vector.

In classification step each class is defined by a representative template represented by n-tuples, which are found in the following manner. Let K sample patterns be elements of the learning set of a class c. The template n-tuples for c are initially set to zero. At the iteration i, where $i = 1...K$, N n-tuples are extracted from the ith sample of the class is being learned, c, resulting in p_i^c. The template n-tuples are updated by a bitwise operation OR. If after i iterations the jth, $j = 1...N$, template n-tuple is $(0, 0, x, ..., x)$, where

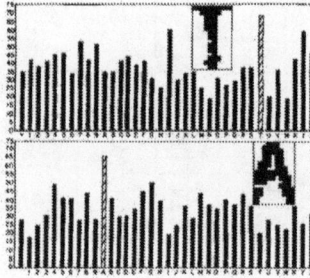

Figure 2.91: Proximity scores for letters 'T' and 'A' [12].

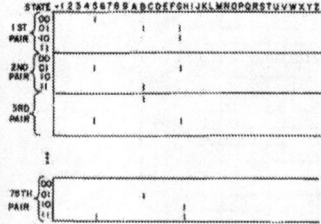

Figure 2.92: Templates for characters 'B', 'G', '5' [12].

$x = 0, 1$, and if the jth, n-tuple extracted from p_{i+1}^c is $(0, 1, x, ..., x)$, the jth template n-tuple will become:

$$(0, 0, x, ..., x) \ OR \ (0, 1, x, ..., x) = (0, 1, x, ..., x)$$

This formula tends to create n-tuples saturated with ones if the data is noisy or if a large learning set presents shape variations within character class [119]. In their original experiment Bledsoe [12] used 75 2-tuples to learn an alphanumeric database. Figure 2.92 shows a set of three templates trained by the system to recognized characters: 'B', 'G', and '5'. In order to classify a new pattern, we only need to compare the feature vector in question to the pre-assembled set of templates. For all stored templates we compare the feature vector is being classified to the template and give it a score based on similarity measure, which is defined in terms of number of corresponding mutually equal positions.

Figure 2.91 shows the "score cards" achieved by the system while classifying printed characters 'T' and 'A'. It is interesting to observe that the scorecard can be used to deduce which characters are most closely related by looking for similar scores. For example, by finding second best score for recognition of character 'T', we can see that character 'I' is its closest match, which we can confirm visually. Analogous relationship can be observed on the second scorecard between characters 'A' and '4'.

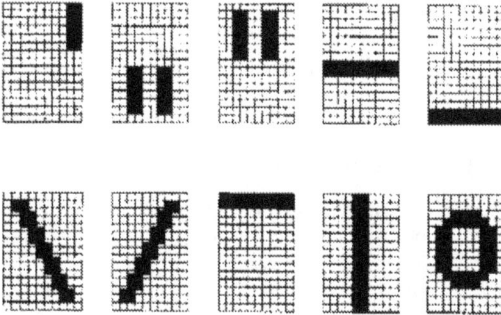

Figure 2.93: 10 basic shapes learned by the system used in [12].

Variety of modifications to the original feature extraction method were presented by Bledsoe [12]. For example, they considered using *non-exclusive* n-tupling scheme where the same sample point can be a part of multiple n-tuples. This resulted in a modest improvement in the overall recognition rate. Additionally, experiments were conducted with multiple values for n, namely: $1, 2, 3, 4$ and 8. Overall tendency of the system was to improve as n increased. If Bledsoe [12] were to try higher order n-tuples, they would see that once n becomes larger than 12, curse of dimensionality sets in and performance drops as reported in Maurycy [119]. Finally meaningful-shape n-tuples were introduced with encouraging results. 10 shapes used by [12] can be seen in figure 2.93.

It is interesting to see a certain level of interest in this feature present till this day; despite its lack of invariance to size and orientation as well as problems it has handling shape variations and noise. Jung *et al.* [84], used N-tuple feature as a part of a generator designed to extract features from any binary character patterns. Such a generator was intended to be used in an automatic universal character recognition system. Systems of that nature are particularly suited for cases where little or no prior information is available about the shape of characters of interest. Additionally, Jung showed that the power of N-tuple feature comes from the fact that it relies on the *difference* in shape between classes of characters, rather than on the shape of character itself.

Anderson and Gaborski [3] have successfully used a variation on the N-tuple feature in their relatively recent work on ZIP code recognition. Presented bellow is a brief outline of features they have extracted.

N-king and N-knight features

Those chess inspired features are an obvious modification of n-tuple method. A detailed description can be found in work of Anderson and Gaborski [3], who found 3-king, 7-king, 5-kinght, and 9 knight to be particularly useful. Just like in the n-tuple method a logical relationship between some pixels in the image is being extracted. The names n-king and n-knight simply refer to the way pixels are chosen in the sampling process.

In chess a king can move by one square in any direction. A knight can move in an 'L' shaped path, which is 2×3 or 3×2 units long. This concept can be generalized to a path of arbitrary length n as indicated by the feature name being prefixed with an integer indicating the size, namely: n-king, and n-knight. By taking an $n \times n$ square, we can take pixels on the perimeter of that square related by stretched king or knight moves. For example, there are four 5-king features, *ai,ck,em,* and *og*, and four 5-king features, *bj, dl, fn,* and *hp*, centered at the '*' as shown bellow:

```
a  b  c  d  e
p  .  .  .  f
o  .  *  .  g
n  .  .  .  h
m  l  k  j  i
```

In order for the above idea to work in general case, n must be even for the n-king North-South and East-West features to be defined. n must also be of the form $4m + 1$ for the n-knight features to be useful [3].

Fuzzy Line features

Another modification of the same idea presented in work of Anderson and Gaborski [3] is the so called fuzzy line feature, which gives rise to *fuzzy-n-knight* and *fuzzy-n-king* features. This time they attempt to get a larger number of pixels contributing to the feature being extracted, by not limiting themselves to a product of just two pixels, but rather a sum of products of multiple pixels. Example they present makes the above idea crystal clear. For the three-by-three square of pixels shown bellow:

```
a  b  c
d  *  f
g  h  i
```

the four fuzzy-3-knight features are: $(a + b)$ x $(h + i)$, $(c + f)$ x $(d + g)$, and $(a + d)$ x $(f + i)$. For a five-by-five example presented above, the four fuzzy-5-features extracted from the perimeter are: $(b + c + d)$ x $(j + k + l)$, $(d+e+f)$ x $(l+m+n)$, $(f+g+h)$ x $(n+o+p)$, and $(h+i+j)$ x $(p+a+b)$.

Anderson and Gaborski report that their fuzzy feature provides a reliable line detection method for lines going through pixel '*' and shows good overall performance. One downside of this method is a very high number of features being extracted, between 600 and 1700 features as indicated in [3]. Fortunately, Anderson and Gaborski provide a way of significantly reducing the number of used features without sacrificing performance. Using a genetic algorithm they evolve a subset of features, which while far fewer in number, still manage to perform at practically the same level. Interested reader is directed to [4] for detailed information.

2.8.3   Shadow Code

First introduced by Burr [20] in 1988 *Shadow Coding* is a popular feature extraction methodology utilized by multiple researchers, see [159, 175, 176, 86, 151, 153, 152, 138] for details. A very similar idea was independently proposed by Lursinsap et al. [115], they called it *Light Receptor Model*. It is not sufficiently different from Shadow Code feature to be given its own

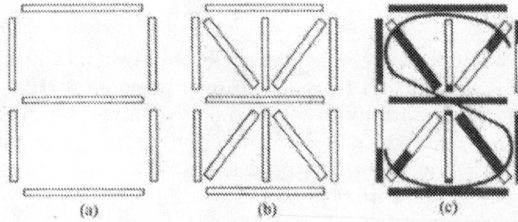

Figure 2.94: (a) Seven-segment bar mask used for digit recognition. (b) 13-segment bar mask used for alphabetic capital letters. (c) illustration of encoding the character 'S' with shadow projections shown in black [20].

section in this book, but interested reader is directed to [115] for detailed description.

A Shadow Code is defined based on a bar mask array like the one shown in Figure 2.94 (a). A simple pattern, such as a digit, can be encoded using just seven-segment bar mask. A more complicated pattern like a letter needs a larger number of bars. Figure 2.94 (b) shows a 13-segment bar mask intended for recognition of capital letters. Finally part (c) of the same Figure is demonstrating the encoding of the character 'S'.

In extracting Shadow-Code-feature an input character is first normalized so it matches the full size of the bar mask. A shadow projection operation is defined, which simultaneously projects a point in the original pattern onto its three closest vertical, horizontal, and diagonal bars. Shadow being cast, turns on a set of bits distributed uniformly along the length of the bar. Once all the points in the original pattern are projected, the number of set-on pixels in each bar is summed up. The character is represented by those n numbers, where n is the number of bars used in the mask [20].

As the result, the pattern is coded in such a way that the shape and structure information are captured and embedded in the resulting code. Although the bars do not touch in the example shown in Figure 2.95 (a), in the actual implementation the bars b_1, b_2 and b_4 intersect at the top-left corner and likewise with the rest of the bars. In order to normalize the feature-vector, we divide the length of the shadowed region by the total length of the bar.

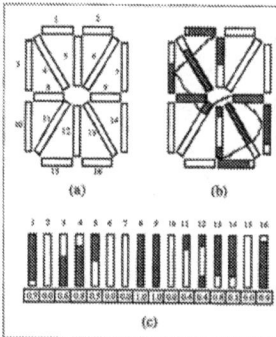

Figure 2.95: (a) 16-bar frame; (b)A binary pattern and corresponding shadows; (c) Normalized Shadow Code [175].

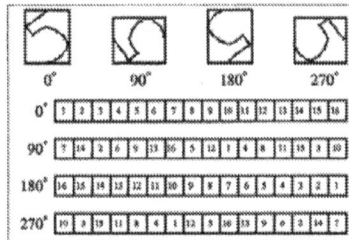

Figure 2.96: Shadow codes for rotations multiple of 90° can be obtained by simply re-ordering the components of the code vector [176].

Shadowed regions can clearly be seen in Figure 2.95 (b). The final normalized shadow vector is shown in Figure 2.95 (c) [175].

In order to simplify the determination of the nearest bar on which the shadow falls, instead of computing the distance from each pixel to each bar we can do the following: divide the rectangle into several domain regions, as indicated by the dashed lines in Figure 2.97, in such a way that the required bar can be found by simply determining in which region a pixel of interest falls. For example in Figure 2.97 (a), there are three dashed lines dividing the rectangle into six regions. A pixel located in the region marked '1' projects its horizontal shadow onto the bar b_1; the vertical shadow will be projected on bar b_3 or b_5 depending on whether the pixel falls in region '3' or '5'; finally its diagonal shadow has to be projected onto bar b_4 [176].

This feature is size independent since the resulting Shadow Code has always the same dimension, as we have to stretch or truncate the input pattern to fit the bar mask properly. In order to achieve rotation invariants for Shadow Code, it is only required to consider the angles, which are multiples of 90°. Due to the shape of the shadow bar frame, the rotated vectors can be easily

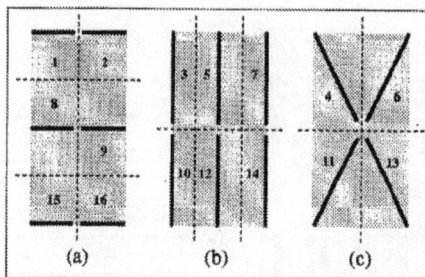

Figure 2.97: Bar domains in which the dashed lines indicate (a) horizontal, (b) vertical, (c) diagonal bars where pixels in each region project their shadows [152].

obtained by changing the order of the vector components as shown in Figure 2.96 [175].

The key step in Shadow Coding is the design of a projection mask that emphasizes the most important structures of the pattern under consideration [86]. As the pattern becomes more complicated, the number of bars in the mask tends to increase in order to capture the inherit complexity of the task. For example, the 32 segment bar mask used by Shirali-Shahreza et al. [159] to encode Persian/Arabic characters is shown in Figure 2.98. The illustration of an Arabic digit '8' encoded using this mask is demonstrated in Figure 2.99.

Extended Shadow Code

An interesting modification of this feature is being used by Sabourin [152] and by Parker [138] for signature verification purposes. They propose combining multiple shadow masks to capture information about an entire signature, they call this approach an *Extended Shadow Coding* and it is demonstrated in Figure 2.100. A great number of possible bar masks used in signature verification shown in Figure 2.101, it demonstrates the great variety of possible encodings inherited in this feature extraction method. The researcher, based on the desired properties being extracted, can select an appropriate mask from the pattern being classified. A deeper description of their approach is not included here as it is beyond the scope of this book.

142

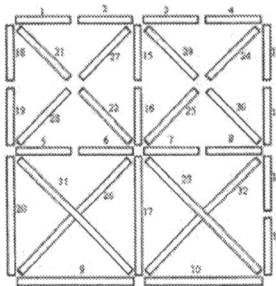

Figure 2.98: 32 segment bar mask [159].

Figure 2.99: Illustration of encoding of Arabic digit '8' using [159].

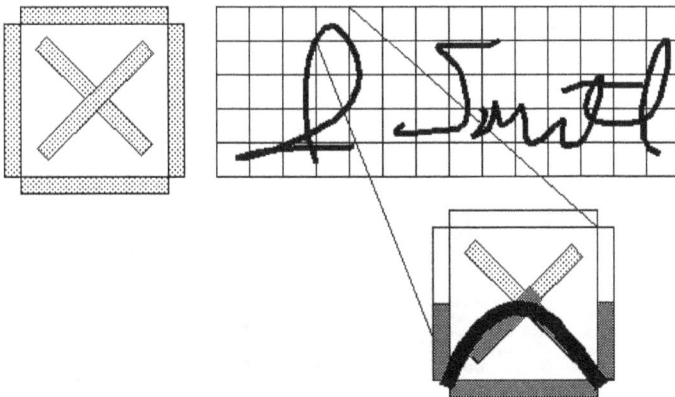

Figure 2.100: Shadow mask for signature verification. Left: An individual sampling square showing the six projection areas to be measured. Right: The signature is drawn over a grid of these squares. Bottom: Each shadow calculation projects the signature in each square onto the projection areas [138].

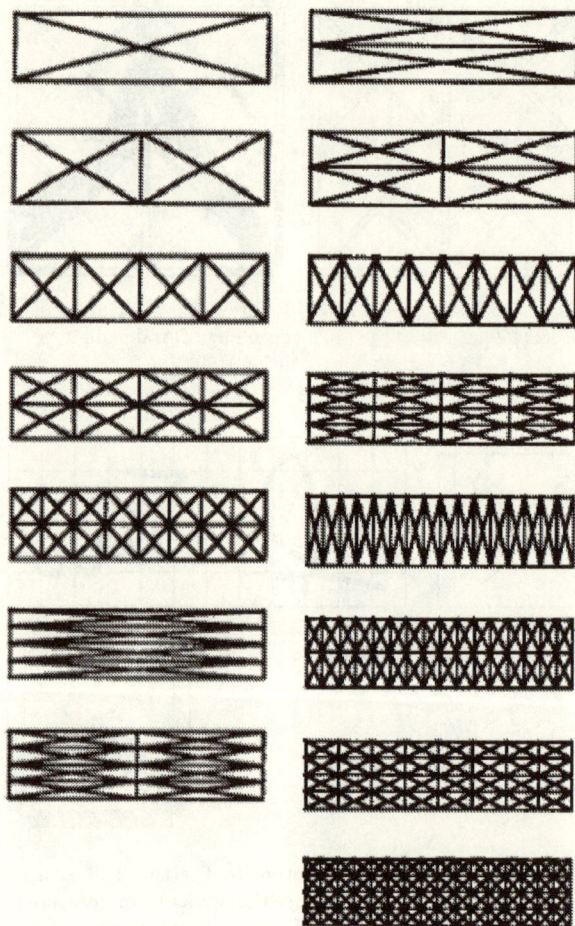

Figure 2.101: Fifteen bar mask representations [152].

2.8.4   Template Matching

This technique is fundamentally different from all other feature extraction methods and so can be in a class by itself. In template matching method, no additional processing is performed and the image itself is used as a feature vector. In the classification stage, a measure of similarity between the image in question and the elements of the set of all templates are calculated. The pattern depicted in the image is assigned the same class as the one to which the most closely matched template belongs. An alternative is to measure the degree of dissimilarity and classify the pattern based on the template with lowest such degree.

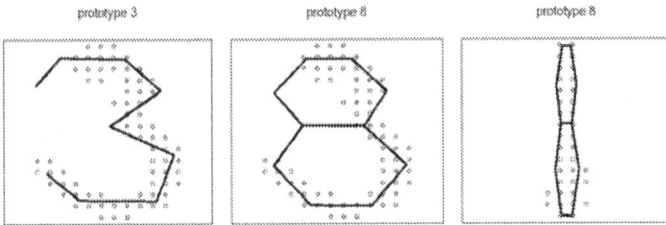

Figure 2.102: Fitting of different templates to the pattern in question [63].

One of the most popular measures of similarity between the gray level patterns and the elements of the template set is the mean square distance:

$$D_j = \sum_{i=1}^{M} (Z(x_i, y_i) - T_j(x_i, y_i))^2 \qquad (2.22)$$

where M is the total number of pixels in Z, the original image and T is the set of all templates. In binary images other similarity measures are used, such as Jaccard and Yule distances [185]. If n_{ij} is the number of pixel positions where the template pixel x is i and the image pixel y is j, with $i, j \in \{0, 1\}$:

$$n_{ij} = \sum_{m=1}^{n} \delta_m(i, j)$$

where

$$\delta_m(i,j) = \begin{cases} 1, & if \ (x_m = i) \wedge (y_m = j) \\ 0, & otherwise \end{cases}$$

$i,j \in \{0,1\}$ and y_m and x_m are the mth pixels of the binary image Y and X. The Jaccard and Yule distances are given as follows:

$$d_J = \frac{n_{11}}{n_{11} + n_{10}n_{01}}$$

$$d_Y = \frac{n_{11}n_{00} - n_{10}n_{01}}{n_{11}n_{00} + n_{10}n_{01}}$$

It is obvious from the definition, that template matching has some serious shortcomings. Templates are only capable of recognizing characters of the same size and rotation and are not tolerant of even smallest variations in shape of the character. Noise in images presents additional problems for template matching. While it is possible to avoid some of the above problems by means of using multiple templates for every type of character, this makes the computational burden on the classification algorithm even greater. Figure 2.103 demonstrates some alternative templates for a small set of digits.

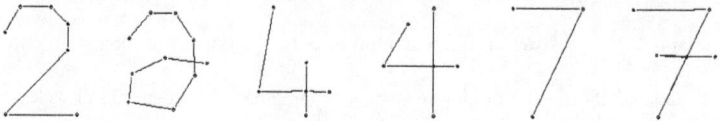

Figure 2.103: Multiple templates for digits with alternative representations [63].

Overall, trivial lock of computational resources large enough to evaluate significant number of templates is what keeps straightforward template matching from becoming more popular.

Deformable Templates

A modified version of Template Matching is well know under the name of *Deformable Templates*. In this approach, the template is not a fixed static structure; rather it is flexible entity, which can be fitted to better match the pattern in question. The degree to which a template can be made to look like the pattern, without changing its morphology, serves as the value based on which the recognition takes place. Algorithm should only change the templates' size and orientation, but not their overall structure.

Figure 2.102 demonstrates fitting of templates for digits '3', '8' and '8' to patterns for digits '3', '3' and '1' respectively. An alternative approach is to morph the pattern in question to make it look as much as possible like the template, while keeping the template static. Figure 2.104 shows how the deformable template approach can be used to recognize a particular pattern, namely digit '6'. Overall this approach is a big improvement over classical template matching as is demonstrated by numerous successful implementations [10, 28, 63, 78, 113, 139].

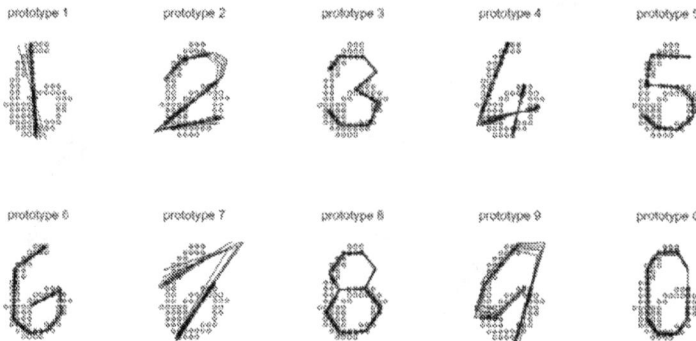

Figure 2.104: Ten templates fitted to an image with pattern in question [63].

Elastic Matching

Not really a feature in itself, *Elastic Matching* (EM) is a classification process closely related to the concept of templates and briefly introduced here for the completeness of presentation. In EM Dynamic Programming, algorithms are used in matching sequences of points with the purpose of measuring similarity between a given set of points and an unknown sample set. The matching is not exact, so only slightly different patterns can be recognized as being essentially the same. This is achieved by using such operations as: insertion and deletion of individual points or even of small sequences of points [156]. Figure 2.105 demonstrates Elastic Matching between a template and an unknown pattern.

Elastic Matching is a relative popular classification approach, which has been used in recognition of handwritten digits [105, 148, 156] and Chinese characters [81]. Its main drawback is relatively high computational cost.

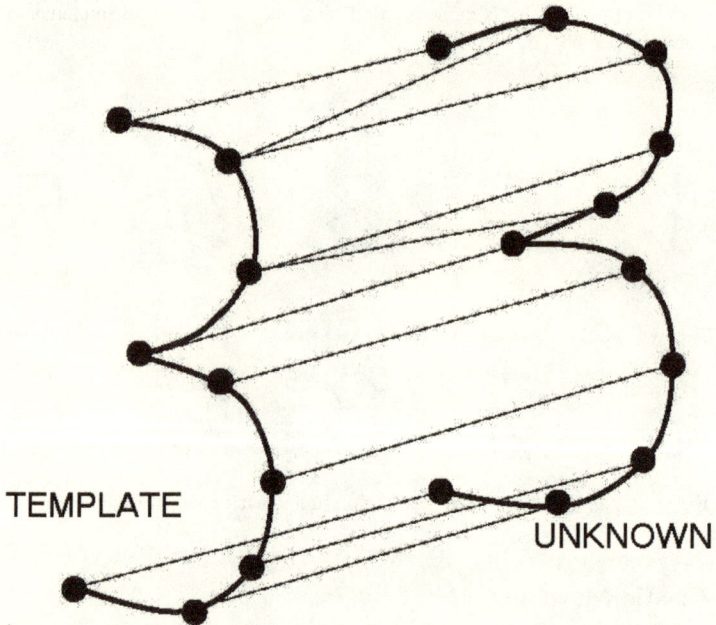

Figure 2.105: Determination of an unknown pattern via point to point distance measurement as performed by Elastic Matching [156].

Chapter 3

Classification Using Neural Network

Knowledge is of two kinds. We know a subject ourselves, or we know where we can find information on it.

Samuel Johnson (1709 - 1784)

3.1 NN for Pattern Recognition

Choice of a classifier is an important factor in recognition type problems such as a character identification. Traditionally statistical classifiers were widely used, but in the last few years *Neural Network* (NN) based approaches are gaining popularity. NN is currently one of the fastest growing research methodologies in science and engineering. New neural network models are being proposed very frequently. While each new type of artificial neural network is being derived as an improvement with respect to prior models, little or no attention is devoted to comparing specific types of networks for particular applications in order to determine the optimal classifier.

Well known NN learning abilities along with the possibility of achieving a high performance due to computational parallelism have resulted in many Optical Character Recognition (OCR) applications based on various NN [53, 55]. In many cases, researchers who are not experts in NN need more advice and practical recommendations on the NN type choice, which for this application area is still not clearly determined. This situation could be explained by difficulty of conducting a theoretical comparison of different NN. The problem might be partly solved by conducting and experimental research and analyzing its results, as was done in this book.

Researcher	Area of Application	MLPN	RBFN
Dong	Satellite Image Classification		Faster running time
Finan	Speaker Recognition		Resilient to bad training data, higher accuracy
Hawickhorst	Speech Recognition		Shorter training time, better retention of generalization capacity
Li	Surgical Decision Making	Statistically insignificant differences	
Lu	Channel Equalization	Fewer Hidden Nodes	Shorter training time, lower error rate
Park	Identification of Nonlinear Dynamics of a Synchronous Generator		Converged closer to a global minimum during the training, required less training time to converge, and fewer computational complexities to train
Roppel	Odor Recognition	Higher Identification Rates	

Figure 3.1: Differences in performance of RBFN and MLPN as reported by different researchers if the field of pattern recognition.

Figure 3.1 depicts the results received by different researchers in various domains, in which MLP and RBF were applied. Based on shown data, one can see that the majority of researchers demonstrate their preferences towards the RBF type networks. Experiments in this study investigate which of the two examined networks is preferable in the area of character recognition.

This chapter compares Multiple Layer Perceptron Network (MLPN) with Radial Basis Function Network (RBFN) in pattern classification applications. Comparison of both theoretical and applied properties of the abovementioned neural networks is conducted based on theoretical analysis of

150

the available results, as well as experiments conducted by the author. An overview of published results shows a significant amount of analysis performed in related areas such as: odder, speech, speaker, and satellite image recognition to name just a few. Figure 3.1 provides a summary of published results, in which MLPN and RBFN are compared.

In recent literature there were a number of publications devoted to the study of how neural networks can be successfully applied to OCR [13, 128] and handwritten character recognition [98, 133]. By studying performance of different NN types in OCR, this book, among its other goals, aims at investigating if the results given in Figure 3.1 could be expanded to character recognition.

For the purposes of this study two very prominent NN types were selected. MLPN was chosen due to its wide spread use and RBFN was selected as its biggest competitor, since in recent years it has quickly gained ground both in terms of its reported performance and amount of utilization.

3.1.1 Multiple Layer Perceptron Network

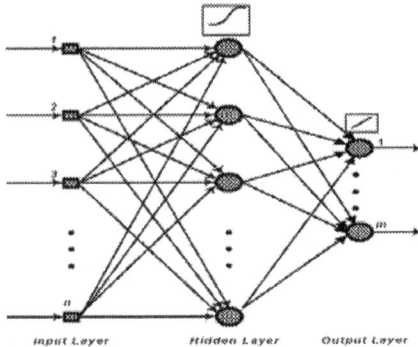

Figure 3.2: Model representation of MLPN.

Multi-Layer Perceptron network is the most popular neural network type.

The MLP network consists of several layers of neurons. Each neuron in a certain layer is connected to each neuron of the next layer. There are no feedback connections. The weights are considered as NN parameters to be adjusted during training. The most often used MLP-network consists of three layers: an input layer, one hidden layer, and an output layer. The hidden and output layers usually have a non-linear activation function. Typically, some type of backpropagation algorithm is used in training this type of network. Figure 3.2 is a model representation of a typical MLPN.

3.1.2   Radial Basis Function Network

A typical Radial Basis Function Network consists of three layers of neurons: input, hidden and output. Each neuron belonging to the hidden layer represents a cluster in the input data space. The hidden layer, as a whole, is a series of such clusters. A radial function, typically Gaussian, serves as an activator for each of the centers. The output for the activation function is determined based on the Euclidian distance between the center and the input vectors. The output neurons calculate a weighted sum of the hidden neurons. Input data values are uniquely assigned to the neurons in the input layer, which pass the data on to the hidden layer directly without any weights. Hidden layer neurons are called RBF units and are determined by a parameter vector called *center* and a scalar value called *width* [11]. Figure 3.3 is a model representation of a typical RBFN.

3.1.3   MLPN vs RBFN

Previous research [41, 47, 52, 154] has pointed to several potential advantages of the MLP neural networks.

1. Unlike the polynomial filter or Gaussian classifier, no assumption is made about the underlying data distribution for designing the MLP networks, so the data statistics do not need to be estimated [119].

2. The MLP network exhibits a great degree of robustness or fault tolerance because of built-in redundancy. Any errors in a few nodes or links thus will not impair overall performance significantly.

3. Implementation of MLP is simple and well documented, due to its popularity, there exist a large number of design packages as well as

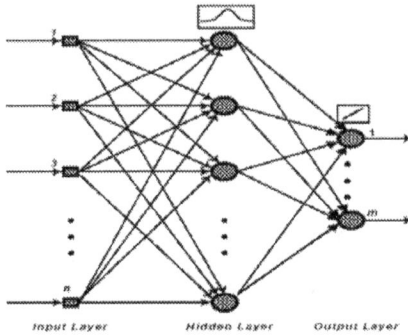

Figure 3.3: Model representation of RBFN.

hardware chips.

Potential advantages of the RBF neural networks include [154]:

1. Local approximation of the data, using only a few hidden units for a given input.

2. Additional control over the network via supplementary parameters.

3. Parameters in the hidden and output layers are trained separately using a fast and efficient hybrid algorithm.

4. Only one hidden layer with full connectivity is used.

5. Hidden layer is non-linear, but output layer is linear.

Chapter 4

Experiment and Program Descriptions

Whatever you can do or dream you can, begin it. Boldness has genius, power, and magic in it.

Johann Wolfgang von Goethe (1749 - 1832)

4.1 Description of Programs

A large number of different programs were created to support the experiments behind this investigative study. They can be roughly divided into five subgroups: data generation, parameter initialization, feature extraction, pattern classification and finally, data analysis. The feature extraction group comprises the largest number of members due to the main topic of this book. A listing of all programs written with short descriptions of their purpose follows:

getData.m Extracts individual digit data from a text file and converts it into usable 1D and 2D forms. Extracts digit labels along the way.

myChain.m Extraction of chain code feature. Number of utilized elements could be constrained. Results are saved in the *chain.out* file.

chain.out Contains the output from the Chain Code feature extraction method.

myCMoment.m Extraction of Central Moments feature. Number of extracted moments could be adjusted.

myConf.m Generates confusion matrix for a particular feature extraction method. Used in analyzing results of experiments.

myDriver.m Controls the experiments. Allows selecting the feature extraction method to be used along with the classifier. Basically, it determines which files from the **my*** library will be run.

myFFT.m Extraction of Fast Fourier Transform feature. Finds a 2D FFT. Number of extracted elements could be changed.

myFractal.m Extraction of the fractal dimension feature. Calculates the fractal dimension using box-counting method. Smallest feature in terms of the size of the resulting feature vector.

myFuzzy.m Extraction of Fuzzy Zoning feature. Number of utilized elements could be constrained. Additionally, Fuzzy Mask could be altered or replaced with another.

myGabor.m Extraction of the Gabor feature from the original pattern. Uses one scale and one orientation. Size of the feature extraction vector could be scaled down as desired.

myHHist.m Extraction of Horizontal Histogram feature.

myHist.m Extraction of Horizontal and Vertical Histogram feature.

myHough.m Extraction of Hough transform feature.

myHu.m Extraction of Hu's 7 moment features.

myMLP.m MLP based classifier used to process extracted feature vector. Also, it reports results of the classification process in an easy to understand summary.

myRBF.m RBF based classifier used to process extracted feature vector. Also, it reports results of the classification process in an easy to understand summary.

myMoment.m Extraction of Geometric moments. Number of extracted moments could be changed.

myNMoment.m Extraction of Normalized Moments. Number of extracted moments could be changed.

myNTuple.m Extraction of the N-tuple feature from the original pattern. 2-tuple is implemented, with the sum of the tuples being used after one of the sample points is multiplied by a factor of 10.

myParams.m Initializes all the variables for controlling the experiment, including size of the training and testing data, size of the feature array and dimensions of input data.

myPixel.m Direct extraction of the individual pixels without any feature extraction method. Serves for comparison purposes and for template matching.

myProfile.m Extraction of Character Profile Feature. Upper, Lower, Left and right character profiles are extracted.

myRandom.m Simulates extraction of the 25D feature from the original pattern. Used as the base measurement in evaluating experiments.

mySimple.m Extraction of Simple 1D Zoning Feature.

mySquares.m Extraction of Concentric Squares Zoning Feature. Center of squares is located in the center of gravity. It automatically determines the maximum possible number of concentric squares based on the location of the center of gravity.

myVHist.m Extraction of Vertical Histogram feature.

myWavelet.m Extraction of the Wavelet Transform feature from the original pattern. Takes the well-known wavelet transform of the given matrix. Daubechies wavelet coefficients are used for wavelet transform operation, which is saved in wavcoeff.mat.

wavcoeff.mat Contains wavelet coefficients for myWavelet.m file.

myZoning.m Extraction of classical Zoning feature.

156

20x30digits.txt Contains all the input patterns in the textual format.

myData.mat Contains all the input patterns extracted from the text file and saved as a Matlab matrix.

   For detailed descriptions of the implemented feature extraction methods, reader is directed towards respective chapters on a particular feature extraction methodology, which usually include a short algorithm outline as well as the basic invariance properties of the approach.

4.2   Data Set Description

All experiments have utilized a library of handwritten digits originally extracted from the US Census forms and postal zip codes. Library is available from Rochester Institute of Technology's public directory maintained by doctor Peter G. Anderson at: www.cs.rit.edu/usr/local/pub/pga/Images/Digits. The selected library consists of over four thousand binarized and manually labeled images, which present a healthy mix of all ten digits from 0 to 9. Digits are represented by a 20 by 30 text matrix, where ones denote background pixels and zeros foreground pixels respectively.

The library was selected for a number of reasons, among them:

- Library is publicly available and is free to use, which makes it easy for others to reproduce my results.

- Digits are extracted from a real-world source, namely US Census forms and US postal zip codes.

- All digits are fully labeled by human evaluators, which results in a very high degree of accuracy.

- Each digit is preprocessed (binarized).

- Library is large enough to allow for the separation of data into multiple groups for training and testing purposes respectively.

   Figures 4.1 and 4.2 demonstrate digits from zero to nine, which are typical of those found in the library. Each digit is followed by a label identifying the character.

```
1111111111111110111  1111111111111111111  1111110000000111111
11111111111111100011 1111111111111111111  11111000000000111111
11111111111111000011 1111111111111111111  1110000000000001111
11111111111110000001 11111111111111000111 1110000000000000111
11111111111100000011 11111111110000000011 110000001100000000111
11111111111100000011 11111111100000000011 10000011111111110000111
11111111111100000011 1111111110000010000l 100001111111111000011
11111111111100000011 11111111111111110001 110001111111111000011
11111111111000001111 11111111111111110001 111111111111110000111
11111111100000111111 11111111111111110011 11111111111000000111
11111111110000011111 11111111111111100011 111111111100000001111
11111111110000011111 11111111111111100011 111110000000000111111
11111111110000011111 11111111111111000011 11000000000001111111
11111111110000011111 11111111111110000111 100000000000011111111
11111111100000111111 1111111100000010000l 000000000000001111111
11111111100001111111 11111000010000011111 110000111000000011111
11111111100001111111 11110000110000011111 11111111111100001111
11111111100001111111 11000011100011111111 11111111111100001111
11111100000011111111 10001110000111111111 11111111111110001111
11111110000011111111 00001000011111111111 11111111111110001111
11111110000011111111 00000000011111111111 11111111111100001111
11111110000011111111 00000011111111111111 11111111111110001111
11111100000011111111 10001111111111111111 11111111111100001111
11111000001111111111 1111111111111111111  11111111110000011111
11111000001111111111 1111111111111111111  11111111100000111111
11110000111111111111 1111111111111111111  11111111000000111111
11100000111111111111 1111111111111111111  1111000000001111111
11000001111111111111 1111111111111111111  10000000001111111111
11000001111111111111 1111111111111111111  11000011111111111111
11000011111111111111 1111111111111111111  1111111111111111111
1111111111111111111  1111111111111111111  1111111111111111111
1                    2                    3

1111111111111111111  1111111111111111111  1111111111111111111
1111111111111111111  11111111111110000111 1111111111111111111
1111111111111111111  11111111111110000011 11111111111110001111
1111111111111111111  11111111111110000001 1111111111111111001111
11111111111111111011 1111111111100000000l 1111111111111100000111
11111111111111110011 11111111100000000011 11111111111110000011
1111111111111110001  11111111100000011011 11111111111100001111
1111111111111110011  11111110000001111111 11111111111100000111111
111110011111111110011 11111100000011111111 11111111110000011111
1111100111111111100011 11110000001111111111 111111110000011111
11110011111111110001 11100000011111111111 11111110000011111
111000111111110001  11100000111111111111 11111110000011111
110001111111111001111 110000011111111111 11111100000111111
1100111111111110001111 1100000011111111111 11111000001111100011
10001111111111001111 11000000111111111111 11110000011000000011
10011111111110000111 11100000001111111111 11100001100000000011
00011111111100000111 11111100000001111111 11000011000000000111
00000000000000011111 11111111100000001111 11000010000000001111
10000000000000011111 111111110000000011 10000000000000011111
1110000010001111111 11111111100000001111 10000000000000011111
11111111110001111111 11111111111100000111 0000000000000011111111
11111111110001111111 11111111111100000111 10000000000011111111
1111111100011111111  11111111110000000111 10000000011111111111
1111111000111111111  111111110000000111  1000011111111111111
111111100011111111   11111110000000011   10000111111111111111
11111100111111111    11110000000001111   10000111111111111111
111111001111111111   10000000001111111   11011111111111111111
1111111111111111111  11000001111111111   11111111111111111111
1111111111111111111  1111111111111111111 1111111111111111111
1111111111111111111  1111111111111111111 1111111111111111111
1111111111111111111  1111111111111111111 1111111111111111111
4                    5                    6
```

Figure 4.1: Examples of digits 1 through 6 from the data set utilized.

```
11111111111111111111 11111111111111111111
11111111111111111111 11111111111000111111
11111111111111111111 11111111100000011111
11111111000000000011 11111111000000001111
11111100000000000011 11111111000111000111
11110000000000000011 11111110011111100111
11110000001111100011 11111100111111100111
11110001111111000011 11111100111111100011
11111111111111000011 11111100111111100011
11111111111111000011 11111100111111100011
11111111111110000111 11111001111111001111
11111111111000001111 11111100111100011111
11111111110000011111 11111100111000111111
11111111110000111111 11111110011000011111
11111111000011111111 11111110000001111111
11111111000111111111 11111110000111111111
11111100001111111111 11111100001111111111
11111000011111111111 11111000001111111111
11110000111111111111 11100001001111111111
11000011111111111111 11100011001111111111
11000011111111111111 11000111001111111111
10000111111111111111 10001111001111111111
00000111111111111111 10011110101111111111
00001111111111111111 00011110011111111111
10111111111111111111 00011100111111111111
11111111111111111111 00000000111111111111
11111111111111111111 10000000111111111111
11111111111111111111 11001111111111111111
11111111111111111111 11111111111111111111
11111111111111111111 11111111111111111111
7                     8
```

```
11111111111111111111 11111111111111111111
11111111111111111111 11111111111111111111
11111111111111111111 11111111111111111111
11111111111111000111 11111111111111111111
11111111111100000011 11111111111111111111
11111111110000000011 11111111111111100111
11111111110001110011 11111111111111100011
11111111100011110011 11111111110000000011
11111111000111110011 11111111110000000111
11111110001111110011 11111111110000000111
11111100111110001111 11111111100000001111
11111000111100001111 11111111000010000111
11111001111000011111 11111110000111001111
11111000000000111111 11111110000111001111
11111000000001111111 11111100001111001111
11111111000011111111 11100001111110001111
11111111000111111111 11100011111110001111
11111110000111111111 11000011111110001111
11111000111111111111 10000111111100011111
11110001111111111111 10001111111000111111
11100011111111111111 00011111110000111111
11000011111111111111 00011111100001111111
10001111111111111111 00000000000111111111
10011111111111111111 10000000011111111111
10111111111111111111 11100011111111111111
11111111111111111111 11111111111111111111
11111111111111111111 11111111111111111111
11111111111111111111 11111111111111111111
11111111111111111111 11111111111111111111
11111111111111111111 11111111111111111111
9                     0
```

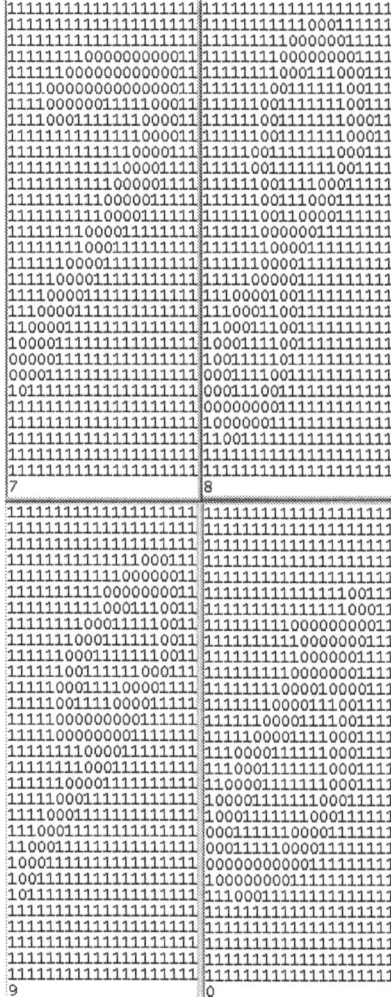

Figure 4.2: Examples of digits 7, 8, 9 and 0 from the data set utilized.

159

4.3 Description of Experiments

Initial experiments were aimed at choosing the network type, which is more appropriate for the area of character recognition. Experiments were designed to facilitate comparison against the following criteria:

- Percentage of accurately recognized digit patterns in never before seen data sets.

- Training time required by the NN to learn to properly discriminate patterns of interest.

- Time required by the NN to recognize a particular instance of a digit.

Simulation was implemented using Matlab's Neural Networks Toolbox (NNT) version 3.0, which is one of the best-known NN simulators. NNT was applied, because its widespread availability makes the experiments easily reproducible by any interested party.

In the case of MLPN the transfer function, which was used is called *tansig*, it is a hyperbolic tangent sigmoid transfer function defined as: $n = 2/(1 + exp(-2 * n)) - 1$. In order to better train the network advantage was taken of Matlab's *trainbr* network training function, which updates the weights and biases according to Levenberg-Marquardt optimization algorithm. It minimizes a combination of squared errors and weights and then it determines the correct combination so as to produce a network, which has good generalizing ability. That process is called Bayesian regularization. Trainbr can train any network if its weight, net input, and transfer functions have derivative functions [196].

Initially, an attempt was made to bypass the feature extraction step, but since that resulted in 20 x 30 = 600 inputs the performance of the networks were sub-optimal with respect to training time. In order to achieve a reasonable training time for the networks, the feature extraction algorithm described above has been used for decreasing the total number of inputs to just 25 signals going into the input layer. This reduction helped to lower the overall complexity of the problem, while maintaining the accuracy levels at around industry standards [162]. Since the ultimate goal was to directly compare MLPN with RBFN the first step had to be determination of individual parameters, which would optimize performance of each network type.

4.3.1 Experiment 1: Optimization of MLPN

In this and other experiments described below, 25 inputs were used, as it is the size of the feature vector produced by the Fuzzy Zoning feature extraction approach. The number of outputs was based on the possible number of different digits and so was set to ten. For all optimization experiments data set of size 2500 was used. All experiments were repeated multiple times to insure that the consistent results have been achieved and that they are reproducible. For each new investigation, the parameters were optimized based on the results already available from the previous experiments.

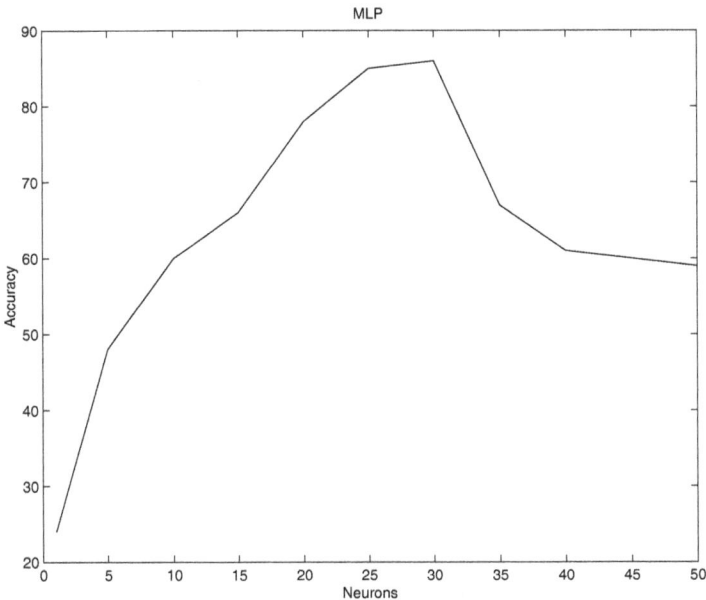

Figure 4.3: Recognition accuracy in percentages (vertical-axis) achieved by MLP based on the number of hidden nodes used.

In case of the MLPN an attempt to boost its recognition accuracy by finding optimal parameters for its topology was made. First, determination of the optimal number of neurons in the hidden layer was performed. By simulating NN with the number of neurons in the range of 1 to 50, it was discovered that the best results came from having about 25 neurons in the hidden layer. Figure 4.3 shows how accuracy of MLPN varies with a changing number of hidden nodes and also demonstrates a strong performance peak in the 25-node region.

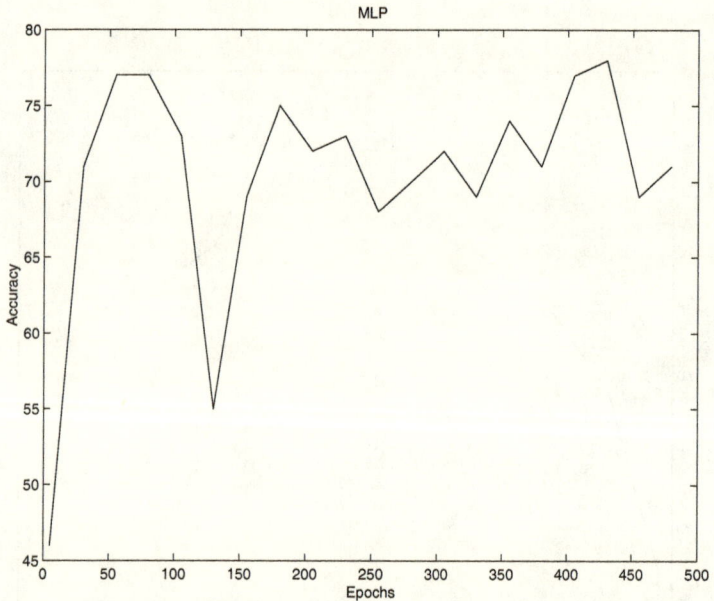

Figure 4.4: Recognition rate in percentages (vertical-axis) achieved by MLP based on the number of training epochs used.

The other parameter, which could be tweaked to improve MLPN's perfor-

mance, was the number of epochs used to train the network. By evaluating
number of epochs in the range of 1 to 500, it was discovered that the best results came from about 50 training epochs. Figure 4.4 shows how accuracy of
MLPN varies with changing number of training epochs and also demonstrates
a relative performance pick in the 50-epoch region. Finally, an attempt to
find the optimal learning rate - Alpha and best performing value for the momentum rate - Beta was made. Figure 4.5 demonstrates the performance of
MLPN based on the value of Alpha (solid line) and Beta (dashed line).

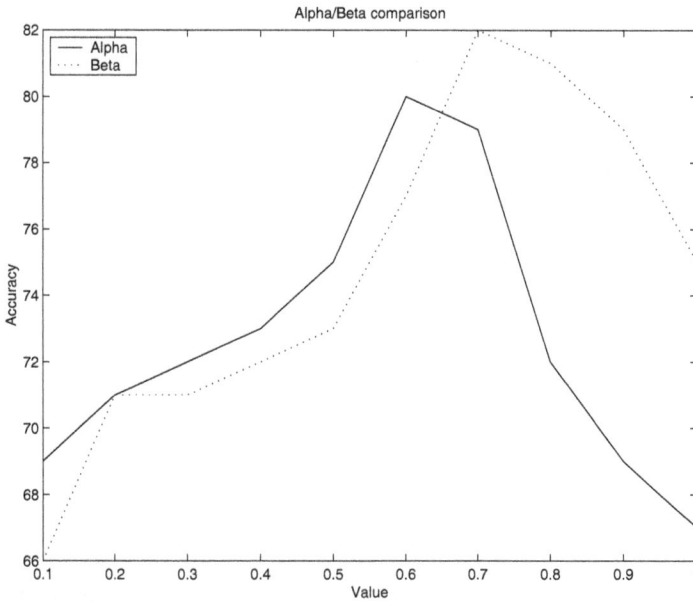

Figure 4.5: Recognition rate in percentages (vertical-axis) achieved by MLP
based on the Alpha/Beta value used.

4.3.2 Experiment 2: Optimization of RBFN

As far as optimization of RBFN is concerned, varying the width parameter of radial basis functions in the range of one to thirty resulted in best performance at the spread level of 10. Figure 4.6 shows an unquestionable single peak in accuracy at the spread value of 10, under which an accuracy of above 90 percent was achieved.

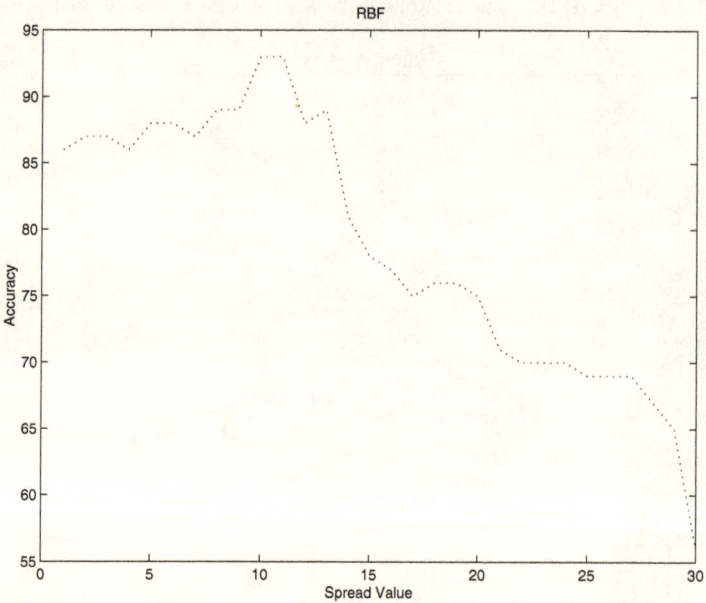

Figure 4.6: Percentage of accurate recognition (vertical-axis) achieved by RBFN based on width of radial basis centers.

4.3.3 Experiment 3: Performance Comparison

This experiment was aimed at determining the neural network type, which performed better with respect to accurate character recognition. In order to establish, which network is more suited for the problem at hand, each network was tested on successively larger training sets, logging which network showed superior performance.

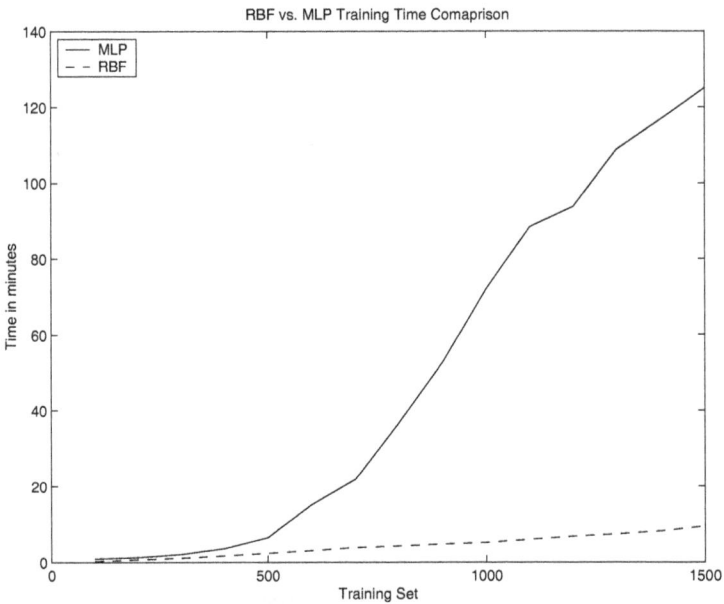

Figure 4.7: Time required by MLPN and RBFN to fully train, based on the size of the training set.

Specifically, after both of the networks were set up with their respective optimal parameters, (MLPN - 25 neurons in the hidden layer and 50 training epochs, RBFN - spread value of 10) determined in previous experiments, and the training process was started. Data set was randomly split into two groups with approximately two-to-one ratio, used for training and testing respectively. Specifically, each network's performance was tested after training them with data sets in the range of 100 to 2500 data elements as depicted in Figure 4.8. This figure compares performance of MLPN vs RBFN on the training sets ranging in size from 100 to 2500 elements with respect to recognition accuracy. RBFN shows a superior performance at all sampling points.

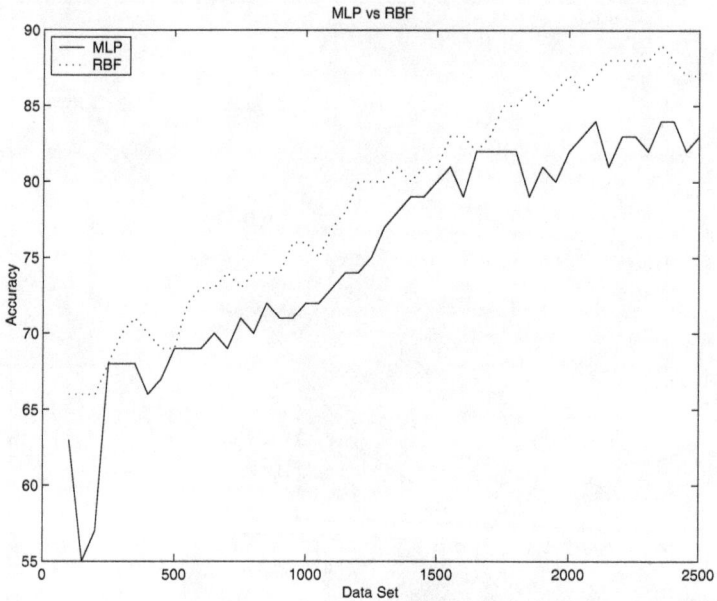

Figure 4.8: Performance of MLPN vs RBFN on the training sets ranging in size from 100 to 2500 elements (horizontal-axis) with respect to recognition accuracy in percentages.

After evaluating the training/testing cycle the following results were achieved; which are given in Figures 4.9 and 4.10 and summarized bellow. Figure 4.9 describes experiments performed with MLPN and aimed at investigating an influence of different factors on recognition accuracy and NN's training time.

Figure 4.10 describes experiments performed with RBFN and aimed at investigating the influence of the training set size and spread factor on recognition accuracy and training time.

#	What is investigated:	# of Experiments	Range Investigated	Minimum Value Achieved	Maximum Value Achieved
	MLPN optimization and evaluation experiments.				
1	Effect of number of hidden nodes on accuracy.	10	1-50	22%	85%
2	Effect of number of training epochs on accuracy.	20	1-500	46%	77%
3	Effect of learning rate on accuracy	10	.1-1	69%	80%
4	Effect of momentum rate on accuracy	10	.1-1	66%	82%
5	How the size of training set effects the training time.	15	100-1500	0Min	125Min
6	How the size of training set effects the accuracy.	50	100-2500	55%	83%

Figure 4.9: MLPN performance statistics.

#	What is investigated:	# of Experiments	Range Investigated	Minimum Value	Maximum Value
	RBFN optimization and evaluation experiments.				
1	Effect of spread value on accuracy.	30	1-30	57%	93%
2	How the size of training set effects the training time.	15	100-1500	0Min	10Min
3	How the size of training set effects the accuracy.	50	100-2500	67%	88%

Figure 4.10: RBFN performance statistics.

1. **Training Time:** RBF had a very strong advantage over MLP against this criterion. In most cases it took approximately ten times less time to train RBF than MLP. In particular for data sets of relatively large size,

training time for MLP was significantly over 2 hours, while RBF took no more than 15 minutes. Figure 4.7 shows the relationship between the size of the data set, and the training time required by each neural network type on training sets of up to 1500 characters.

2. **Recognition Time:** In the experiments no statistically significant differences between recognition time required by MLP versus the time required by RBF was found. This could be explained in part by peculiarities of the NN implementation utilized in Matlab's NN toolbox.

3. **Recognition Accuracy:** To measure accuracy the percentage of correctly recognized never before seen digits for each network type was computed. Regardless of the size of training set, RBFN outperformed, or did at least as well as MLPN.

4.3.4 Conclusions with respect to MLPN and RBFN

Theoretical investigation and experimental study of the choice of the NN type for application in pattern recognition has been conducted and resulted in practical recommendations on NN type and parameter selection. Most popular MLP and RBF were compared against criteria of recognition accuracy, training and recognition time. Both types were initially optimized before comparison was performed, in total more than 250 experiments have been conducted. Figures 4.9 and 4.10 summarize all the performed experiments.

The study demonstrated the advantage of the RBFN against both recognition accuracy and training time criteria with the gain of about 10 to 20 percent in recognition accuracy and a very significant gain in training time. Experiments performed did not allow getting statistically significant difference in recognition time. The results allow recommending an application of RBFN for alphanumerical character recognition, as well as in adjacent areas of pattern recognition. The RBF spread factor parameter should be chosen around value 10. Experiments demonstrate that 10-fold increase in the training set size requires 10 times more time for training but results in about two times increase in recognition accuracy.

Chapter 5

Summary of Results

Knowledge is power.

Sir Francis Bacon (1561 - 1626)

5.1 Taxonomy of Features

This book clearly shows how human ingenuity has translated into dozens of different feature extraction methodologies (FEM). New features are constantly being proposed and old ones improved upon by many researchers. In order to better understand the direction of future developments as well as to be able to more honestly compare different features, classification of feature extraction methods themselves is necessary.

The general majority of known feature extraction methods can be classified into four broad distinct categories, namely:

- *Image itself* - perfectly describes the pattern, but is computationally too demanding, and so makes classification very difficult.

- *Distributions* - statistical features of the pattern, such as area, center of mass, pixel count in sub-windows and so on.

- *Series expansion coefficients* - pattern represented as an infinite series, such as Fourier, Walsh, or Cosinus. A small subset of all terms is being taken and their coefficients are used as features.

- *Structural features* - the pattern is being described in terms of its comprising features at a higher level, for example loops, strokes, end points, etc [119].

Many researchers have proposed more involved taxonomy structures for classifying different types of feature extraction methods. Fisher [48] suggests an all inclusive taxonomy of geometric features, which contains well over a hundred different approaches. His taxonomy could be found in the Appendix - A located in Chapter 7.

A more limited in size and in scope classification approach is shown in the work of Trier et al. [185]. In their approach, the features are subdivided into four groups based on the type of character pattern they are applied to. Those types are: gray scale patterns, binary solid characters and binary outer contours of the character, and finally, vector representations or skeletons of the pattern. Figure 5.1 demonstrates classification of some eleven features into those four groups, with some features being assigned to more than one group.

Gray scale subimage	Binary		Vector (skeleton)
	solid character	outer contour	
Template matching	Template matching		Template matching
Deformable templates			Deformable templates
Unitary Transforms	Unitary transforms		Graph description
	Projection histograms	Contour profiles	Discrete features
Zoning	Zoning	Zoning	Zoning
Geometric moments	Geometric moments	Spline curve	
Zernike moments	Zernike moments	Fourier descriptors	Fourier descriptors

Figure 5.1: Classification of feature extraction methods for the various character representation forms [185]

Laaksonen [94] expanded on the work above and added some additional four features to the classification scheme. He has also rearranged and grouped the features. In figure 5.2 five subgroups can be seen, namely: templates, transforms and moments, descriptors and codes, discrete features and finally, zoning is in a group by itself.

feature extraction	Gray-scale subimage	Binary solid symbol	Binary outer contour	Vector skeleton
			representation form	
Template matching	X	X		X
Deformable templates	X			X
Unitary transforms	X	X		
Log-polar transform *	X	X		
Geometric moments	X	X		
Zernike moments	X	X		
Wavelets *	X	X		
Algebraic features *	X	X		
Projection histograms		X		
Fitted Masks *	X	X		
Contour profiles			X	
Chain codes			X	
Spline curve			X	
Fourier descriptors			X	X
Graph description				X
Discrete features				X
Zoning	X	X	X	X

Figure 5.2: Features from taxonomy by Trier, but rearranged and grouped and methods marked with an asterisk have been added [94].

A smaller subgroup of features is taken by Laaksonen and arranged in
a different fashion, as can be seen in Figure 5.3. Transforms, moments,
wavelets, algebraic features, and histograms are grouped under the title *Volume* features. Excluded features are template matching, deformable templates, and zoning [94].

	structural	statistical
heuristic	• Discrete features	• Fitted masks
systematic	• Chain codes • Spline curve • Graph description	• Volume features • Contour profiles • Fourier descriptors

Figure 5.3: A dichotomy 'strucural' versus 'statistical' reflects the corresponding principles of classification. The words 'heuristic' and 'systematic'
refer to the way the features are selected [94]

The heuristic methods are based on some properties, which are found
useful in the classification of a particular type of characters, often based on
research in human perception. The systematic methods are more rigorous
and try to describe the character in precise mathematical terms. Structural
methods work well with tree-based classifiers or with sets of rules. Statistical ones are well suited for neural networks or some traditional classifiers [94].

In this work the author has grouped the features into seven different somewhat interrelated sets. They are shown in the Figure 5.4 with some but
definitely not all the known features placed in their respective sets.

While many features and feature modifications are not yet listed in Figure
5.4, it is believed that any not yet listed feature could be classified without
addition of a new class to the taxonomy, particularly due to inclusion of
the *Miscellaneous* group. It is also possible to get a more general classification by reassigning Fractal Based Features to the Transform group and the
Histogram Based approaches to the Structural group, resulting in only five
different sets.

Feature Classification	Included Examples
Image Partitioning Approaches	Zoning, Fuzzy Zoning, Meta-Zoning, Angular Partitions, Radial Coding, Track and Sectors
Histogram Based Approaches	Vertical and Horizontal Projection Histograms, Ring Projections
Method of Moments	Geometric, Central, Normalized, Transformed, Radial, Angular, Gegenbauer, Legendre, Tchebichef, Krawtchouk, Zernike, Pseudo-Zernike, Fourier-Mellon
Structural Approaches	Structural Features, Feature Points, Strokes, Character Profiles, Graph Descriptions, Crossing Methods
Transform Based Approaches	Fourier, Gabor Filter, Hough, Chain Code Transform, Wavelet Transform
Fractal Based Approaches	Fractal Encoding, Fractal Feature
Miscellaneous Approaches	Characteristic Loci, N-Tuples, Shadow Codes, Templates

Figure 5.4: A taxonomy proposed by the author for the feature extraction methods utilized in character recognition.

5.2   Summary of Results

Previous chapters introduced the reader to the FEMs described in the literature, often alongside the results achieved by the investigators. However, the performance of different approaches could not be directly compared since different sets of data were used in almost all the experiments.

In this chapter, FEMs from seven sets described in the taxonomy section above are implemented and their performance is reported. They are all compared against the same data set, which is good since it keeps the comparison fair, but also might be bad since the data might be best suited for a particular feature extraction methodology. The same goes for the classifier as well. Neural network, namely RBFN, is used to classify all features with same pros and cons as above to be considered. Overall, author has decided that fundamental fairness of comparison outweighs any bias a data set or a classifier may have towards a particular feature extraction approach.

Initially MLPN was supposed to be a second classifier, but after experiments showed that it is an inferior recognizer and same conclusion was found in literature (see Chapter 4) it was decided not to use MLP as a classifier all together. The fact that MLPN tended to run out of memory and took almost ten times longer to accomplish the same task as RBFN was also a contributing factor.

For the recognition experiments data set was divided into four groups a thousand characters each. Classifier was trained on the three thousand characters and tested on the fourth. The fourth thousand used for testing was switched places with each of the thousand-character-sets used in the process of training. The average performance in all four cases was taken as the final accuracy of the feature. This approach is know as *leave-one-out* method.

Figure 5.5 demonstrates a classified listing of tested feature extraction methods along with the accuracy achieved by each one and the size of the feature vector produced. It can be seen that the recognition accuracy of our character recognition system can change from as little as 16.2 percent to as much as 91.6 percent depending on the feature extraction method. Variance just as great can be seen in the size of the extracted feature vectors, which range from just 1 to the size of the original input pattern (600).

Feature Extraction Method	Accuracy in Percentages	Size of Feature Vector
Image Partitioning Approaches		
1D Zoning	60.4	25
2D Zoning	91.6	25
Fuzzy Zoning (linear mask)	84.7	25
Fuzzy Zoning (quadratic mask)	66.9	25
Center of Pattern Zoning (Concentric Squares)	43.2	9
Center of Image Zoning (Concentric Squares)	41.6	9
Histogram Based Approaches		
Vertical Histogram	43.2	20
Horizontal Histogram	71.2	30
Vertical and Horizontal Histogram	71.7	50
Method Of Moments		
Geometric Moments	53.4	15
Central Moments	48.1	15
Normalized Moments	41.2	15
Hu's Moments	36.6	7
Structural Approaches		
Character Profiles	79.9	100
Transform Based Approaches		
Hough Transform	88.6	25
Chain Code Transform	42.4	100
Gabor Filter	76.2	600
Fast Fourier Transform	72.3	600
Wavelet	46.9	400
Fractal Based Approaches		
Fractal Dimension (box counting)	16.2	1
Other Approaches		
Direct Pixel Matching	71.1	600
N-tuple	60.2	20
Randomly Generated Feature (for testing)	10 (average)	25

Figure 5.5: Listing of tested feature extraction methods with achieved accuracy and size.

Figure 5.5 illustrates performance of tested feature extraction methodologies, while keeping the features grouped based on the taxonomy proposed by the author. It might be helpful to look at the ranking of features not considering their class, but solely based on their performance. Figure 5.6 organizes feature extraction techniques based on the shown recognition accuracy from best performing to worst performing.

Feature Extraction Method	Accuracy in Percentages
2D Zoning	91.6
Hough Transform	88.6
Fuzzy Zoning (linear mask)	84.7
Character Profiles	79.9
Gabor Filter	76.2
Fast Fourier Transform	72.3
Vertical and Horizontal Histogram	71.7
Horizontal Histogram	71.2
Direct Pixel Matching	71.1
Fuzzy Zoning (quadratic mask)	66.9
1D Zoning	60.4
N-tuple	60.2
Geometric Moments	53.4
Central Moments	48.1
Wavelet	46.9
Center of Pattern Zoning (Concentric Squares)	43.2
Vertical Histogram	43.2
Chain Code Transform	42.4
Center of Image Zoning (Concentric Squares)	41.6
Normalized Moments	41.2
Hu's Moments	36.6
Fractal Dimension (box counting)	16.2
Randomly Generated Feature (for testing)	10 (average)

Figure 5.6: Listing of tested feature extraction methods sorted by accuracy.

Another very important property of the feature is the size of the feature vector itself. Smaller feature vectors allow for much faster classification as well as reduce the burden on the available computer memory. Figure 5.7 organizes feature extraction techniques based on the respective size from smallest to largest. It is important to keep in mind that with any feature, the size of the feature vector can always be reduced by not including some elements. Obviously, this can result in the reduced recognition accuracy.

Feature Extraction Method	Size of Feature Vector
Fractal Dimension (box counting)	1
Hu's Moments	7
Center of Pattern Zoning (Concentric Squares)	9
Center of Image Zoning (Concentric Squares)	9
Geometric Moments	15
Central Moments	15
Normalized Moments	15
Vertical Histogram	20
N-tuple	20
1D Zoning	25
2D Zoning	25
Fuzzy Zoning (linear mask)	25
Fuzzy Zoning (quadratic mask)	25
Hough Transform	25
Randomly Generated Feature (for testing)	25
Horizontal Histogram	30
Vertical and Horizontal Histogram	50
Character Profiles	100
Chain Code Transform	100
Wavelet	400
Gabor Filter	600
Fast Fourier Transform	600
Direct Pixel Matching	600

Figure 5.7: Listing of tested feature extraction methods sorted by respective size of the feature vector.

5.3   Normalized Accuracy Measure

The measure of accuracy as shown in the Figures 5.5 and 5.6 is determined by simply taking the percentage of accurately recognized characters from all the cases being tested. While this approach does unambiguously demonstrate the overall performance of the pattern recognizing system, it is not an objective measure of performance by a particular feature extraction methodology since it does not take into account the size of the feature vector.

This is clearly a problem as can be demonstrated with a simple but exaggerated example. Suppose feature X has recognition accuracy of 86 percent and consists of a 35D feature vector. Another feature, Y, has recognition accuracy of 94 percent, but consists of a 136D feature vector. Which feature is showing a better performance? The approach usually taken by most researchers is simply to select the best performing feature in absolute sense, in this case X.

Another approach would be to truncate feature vectors from all feature extraction approaches to the same size and do the direct comparison based on recognition ability of resulting feature vectors. So in the case of our ongoing example we might truncate Y to be same size as X, namely 35D. It would not be to surprising if the performance of Y dropped significantly as the result, to perhaps as little as 37 percent. Under this methodology feature X, shows superior performance. This is a problem since this methodology is highly biased against large feature arrays. Some features require a certain dimensionality in order to achieve a particular level of performance, so this approach is not a feasible solution to our feature comparison problem.

The alternative approach, Normalized Accuracy Measure (NAM), proposed by the author does not artificially restrict the size of the feature vectors; rather it takes into account their dimensionality in calculating the discriminatory ability of the feature. NAM is defined as absolute accuracy achieved by the feature divided by the dimensionality of the feature vector. In case of our example NAM of X is 2.46 and NAM of Y is .69. Clearly X is a superior feature extractor per unit of information.

Figure 5.8 shows listing of tested feature extraction methods sorted by Normalized Accuracy Measure from highest to lowest.

178

Feature Extraction Method	Normalized Accuracy (%)
Fractal Dimension (box counting)	16.2
Hu's Moments	5.22
Center of Pattern Zoning (Concentric Squares)	4.8
Center of Image Zoning (Concentric Squares)	4.6
2D Zoning	3.6
Geometric Moments	3.5
Hough Transform	3.5
Fuzzy Zoning (linear mask)	3.3
Central Moments	3.2
N-tuple	3.0
Normalized Moments	2.7
Fuzzy Zoning (quadratic mask)	2.6
1D Zoning	2.4
Horizontal Histogram	2.3
Vertical Histogram	2.1
Vertical and Horizontal Histogram	1.4
Character Profiles	.8
Chain Code Transform	.42
Randomly Generated Feature (for testing)	.4
Gabor Filter	.12
Fast Fourier Transform	.12
Direct Pixel Matching	.11
Wavelet	.11

Figure 5.8: Listing of tested feature extraction methods sorted by achieved accuracy normalized for the size of the feature vector.

An optional additional step in calculation of NAM may be the subtraction of 100 divided by the number of distinct symbol classes from the absolute accuracy in order to take into account the probability of successfully guessing the character. This step slightly reduces the NAM measure and allows for the possibility of having negative NAM values.

Negative performance is not something a real-world feature extraction approach would ever have, but it is important to include it for sake of mathematical completeness. Assuming in our example we a dealing with recognition of digits, we need to subtract $100/10 = 10$ from absolute accuracy. In this case NAM of X becomes 2.17 and NAM of Y is now .62. Still, X is a superior feature extractor per unit of information.

Figure 5.9 shows listing of tested feature extraction methods with achieved Normalized Accuracy Measure reduced by the average number of accurate character recognitions produced by random guessing. Normalization for random guessing rarely makes a difference in the relative ranking of feature extraction methods, but it does happen sometimes as can be seen highlighted in bold in Figure 5.9 for Geometric Moments and Hough Transform methods. Also, the Randomly Generated Feature has the NAM of 0 under this calculation scheme, which is a desired property of any feature evaluation measure.

The NAM is a valuable tool for unbiased evaluation of feature extraction methods. It provides a single value to represent the quality of a feature. The NAM takes feature size into account and is geared towards rewarding more compact feature representations, while progressively 'punishing' excessively large features as their size increases. In addition, it prevents random guessing from affecting the feature performance. The Normalized Accuracy Measure is also easy to calculate regardless of the type of data set or the number of different character classes included.

Overall, NAM could be thought of as capacity of the feature to describe the pattern in a given unit of information. It is valuable that the zero mark is assigned to the random guessing process as a starting point for evaluating real features. It is also great to observe that as the size of the feature approaches that of original pattern (600) in Figure 5.9, NAM approaches zero.

Feature Extraction Method	Normalized Accuracy (Corrected for random guessing)
Fractal Dimension (box counting)	6.2
Hu's Moments	3.8
Center of Pattern Zoning (Concentric Squares)	3.7
Center of Image Zoning (Concentric Squares)	3.5
2D Zoning	3.3
Geometric Moments	**2.9**
Hough Transform	**3.1**
Fuzzy Zoning (linear mask)	2.9
Central Moments	2.5
N-tuple	2.5
Normalized Moments	2.1
Fuzzy Zoning (quadratic mask)	2.2
1D Zoning	2.0
Horizontal Histogram	2.0
Vertical Histogram	1.7
Vertical and Horizontal Histogram	1.2
Character Profiles	.69
Chain Code Transform	.32
Randomly Generated Feature (for testing)	**0**
Gabor Filter	.11
Fast Fourier Transform	.10
Direct Pixel Matching	.10
Wavelet	.09

Figure 5.9: Listing of tested feature extraction methods with achieved accuracy normalized for the size of the feature vector and for random guessing.

5.4 More on Individual Features

The following sections provide additional details about implemented features as well as some analysis of those features.

5.4.1 Image Partitioning Approaches

All features in this subsection are based on the idea of dividing the pattern into a number of zones of varying shape and calculating the number of foreground pixels in those zones.

1D Zoning

A variation on classical zoning in which a zone is defined as N continuous pixels, instead of a two-dimensional box surrounding a number of image points. Big advantage of this feature is ease of implementation, but since the recognition results turned out to be inferior to classical zoning no additional analysis will be performed.

2D Zoning

This is one of the earliest discovered feature extraction approaches, but it showed excellent performance in comparison to other features examined in this book. A number of additional experiments were performed on this feature due to its successful operation.

First, we tried to determine the influence of the number of zones, out of total 25, on the achieved level of performance. Figure 5.10 shows the results of reducing size of the zoning feature vector. It is amazing to learn just how resilient the zoning feature is to such truncation, particularly in early stages. Twenty percent reduction in size of the zoning feature results in pattern recognition accuracy drop of less than one percent.

Number of Zones	5	10	15	20	25
Accuracy (%)	37.3	62.7	83.4	91.0	91.6

Figure 5.10: Number of 2D zones versus accuracy.

Additionally, taking even as six as five zones shows relatively good recognition accuracy level of over 37 percent. Remembering that zoning is similar to human pattern processing, we would expect that taking the same number of zones in the middle of the pattern, as opposed to the side, would improve resulting performance. Experiment aimed at proving this theory resulted in numbers depicted in Figure 5.11, which clearly demonstrates how performance increases as six taken zones are selected closer towards the middle of the pattern.

Range of Zones	0:5	5:10	10:15	15:20	20:25
Accuracy (%)	37.3	51.5	61.3	46.9	31.0

Figure 5.11: Location of five 2D zones versus accuracy.

Confusion matrix obtained from zoning feature is shown in Figure 5.12.

Zoning		Actual type of pattern:								
		0	1	2	3	4	5	6	7	8	9
	0	88	0	0	1	0	0	0	0	1	0
Classification	1	0	91	1	0	0	0	2	2	0	0
determined	2	0	0	73	4	0	1	0	0	0	0
by the system	3	2	0	8	103	0	8	0	0	9	0
based on	4	0	0	0	0	100	1	0	1	1	0
feature	5	1	0	1	1	0	31	0	0	1	0
extraction	6	3	0	0	0	1	0	109	0	0	0
method:	7	0	0	1	1	1	0	0	113	0	11
	8	0	1	5	1	1	1	0	0	104	0
	9	0	0	0	0	3	0	0	5	2	104

Figure 5.12: Confusion matrix produced by the zoning feature.

By examining Figure 5.12, we can see that the most commonly confused digit pairs as produced by the zoning feature are: '7' - '9', '2' - '3' and '3' - '8'. This is not surprising, as the zoning feature produces results similar to those of a blurred human visual system and to a human the above-mentioned digit pairs do look alike.

Fuzzy Zoning (linear mask)

A variation on zoning feature proposed by the author and aimed at reducing effect of sharp borders between zones by allowing a single pixel to contribute to multiple zones. The actual contribution of the pixel depends on the type of fuzzy mask utilized. In this case a linear mask was used and produced promising results showing performance among the top three features as computed by the simple accuracy measure. It did produce results inferior to the simple 2D zoning, but it might be a result of an under-optimized fuzzy mask. The fact that this feature was used to optimize the classifier used by the pattern recognition system on all other features should be taken into consideration during evaluation of this feature's performance.

Fuzzy Zoning (quadratic mask)

Same as above, but with a quadratic function based mask. This was a result of trying to produce a better fuzzy mask, but unfortunately since the design was done by hand it did not turn out to be any better. Perhaps in future experiments the fuzzy mask could be evolved using a Genetic Algorithm search to produce an optimal set of weight for the Fuzzy Mask.

Center of Pattern Zoning (Concentric Squares)

Same as zoning, but zones are not squares rather they are progressive perimeters from the center of the pattern to the edges of the image. Relatively low recognition accuracy made this feature not valuable in the face of 2D zoning or even Fuzzy zoning.

Center of Image Zoning (Concentric Squares)

Same as above, but the center for concentric squares is not the center of the pattern, but the static center of the image. Performance was inferior to all other zoning approaches.

5.4.2   Histogram Based Approaches

All features in this subsection are based on the idea of projecting the character onto a number of bins in order to get a histogram graph.

Vertical Histogram

Projection of the character onto the row of bins located at the bottom of the character. This feature represents a simple approach with low tolerance for rotation invariance, and consequently mediocre results. Relatively small feature size, but that heavily depends on the width of the input characters, or the chosen number of bins.

Horizontal Histogram

This feature is same as above, but projection is taken along the side of the character with the height of the input pattern equal to the size of the feature vector. This feature is about 50 percent larger than the Vertical Histogram and is respectively better.

Vertical and Horizontal Histogram

This feature is a combination of the Vertical and Horizontal histogram features. The size of this feature is equal to the sum of the two components, but the performance is practically the same as from the Horizontal component alone. So, consequently it has no advantage over the Horizontal histogram and its grater size makes it an inferior feature.

5.4.3 Method Of Moments

All features in this subsection are based on the idea of calculating statistical moments over the 2D pattern.

Geometric Moments

These classical moments are well-established character descriptors, comprising of: mass, center of mass, average energy, skewness, kurtosis, etc. How each increase in the moments order effects achieved recognition can be seen from Figure 5.13. Low order moments can be seen to contain lots of useful information, with higher order moments providing additional support in recognizing character in question.

Overall, acceptable performance was achieved particularly considering only a small number of total moments were extracted. As Figure 5.13 shows, adding

185

additional moments keeps the accuracy growing. For fairness of comparison with other features, no optimal number of moments was searched for.

Number of Geometric Moments	1	3	6	10	15
Moment Order (p + q)	0	1	2	3	4
Accuracy (%)	14.8	29.8	49.4	51.8	53.4

Figure 5.13: Number of Geometric moments versus accuracy.

Normalized Moments

This is feature similar to Geometric moments, but translated with respect to the center of mass and normalized with respect to 0th order geometric moment.

Hu's Moments

This feature consists of a set of seven moments invariant to size, orientation and position. One of the best properties of this feature is a very small size of the feature vector. Performance is very respectable if the small dimensionality of this feature is taken into consideration. As the difference in magnitude between the first and higher order moments could be very dramatic, a normalizing constant needs to be employed to make all moments contribute, at least to some degree, to the final decision of the classifier. The value of such constant can greatly influence performance of this feature. However, since other feature extraction methods were not optimized in any way, it seems to be unfair to try and find the best value for such constant for application with Hu's moments. As a consequence, other researchers who chose to optimize performance of Hu's moments may report slightly better results.

5.4.4   Structural Approaches

The only feature in this subclass is based on the outer boundaries of the character.

Character Profiles

A feature based on the distance from the outer perimeter of the character to the side of the image. Four profiles in total were extracted, namely: Upper, Lower, Left and Right. Their relative performance and their size can be seen from Figure 5.14.

Combination of all four profiles produced the best feature in terms of absolute accuracy, but combining just Left and Upper profiles resulted in good accuracy, considering the savings in the size of the feature in comparison to having all four subfeatures are being combined into a single vector. The size of this feature heavily depends on the size of the input pattern, and in this case ranges from 20 to 100 units of information.

Profile Type	Left	Right	Up	Down	All	Left & Up
Accuracy	71.2	55.3	64.6	54.6	79.9	77.9
Feature Vector Size	30	30	20	20	100	50

Figure 5.14: Accuracy produced by different types of Profile feature.

5.4.5 Transform Based Approaches

All features in this subsection are based on the idea of transforming the image into an alternative mathematical space.

Hough Transform

Feature based on the well established in computer vision concept of Hough Transformation often used for detection of straight lines or with some modifications of circles. Since this feature showed high recognition accuracy in comparison to most other features, its Confusion matrix is shown in Figure 5.15

We can see that the most commonly confused digit pairs as produced by the Hough Transform feature are: '8 - '9' and '2' - '7'; this is consistent with the line detecting ability of the Hough Transform, as the differences between those digits are very close to being a single stroke.

Hough Transform	Actual type of pattern:									
		0	1	2	3	4	5	6	7	8	9
Classification determined by the system based on feature extraction method:	0	88	0	0	1	0	0	0	1	2	0
	1	0	90	2	0	0	0	5	0	3	0
	2	1	0	70	1	0	0	0	2	2	2
	3	1	0	0	104	1	1	0	1	3	2
	4	1	0	0	0	91	0	0	0	1	0
	5	0	0	1	1	0	35	0	0	2	0
	6	0	1	2	0	6	3	106	0	2	0
	7	1	0	8	1	1	0	0	116	2	0
	8	2	1	5	3	1	3	0	0	81	6
	9	0	0	1	0	5	0	0	1	20	105

Figure 5.15: Confusion matrix produced by the Hough Transform feature.

Chain Code Transform

This feature is based on image compression techniques commonly used in computer vision applications. For a relatively large feature vector, it only produced mediocre results.

Gabor Filter

This feature is based on Gabor functions, which are used to model the cells in the mammal's visual cortex system. For a very large feature vector, it only produced second-rate results. The size of this feature can be greatly reduced to improve the performance to size ratio, but not the overall accuracy.

Fast Fourier Transform

This feature utilizes common Fast Fourier Transform function to produce as many FFT points as desired. How the number of such points affects the overall accuracy can be seen in Figure 5.16.

Clearly, as the number of FFT points increases so does the performance of this popular feature. At a reasonable size of about 30 feature points, the accuracy produced is very ordinary.

Number of FFT Samples	10	20	30	40	50	60	600
Accuracy (%)	31.0	40.1	49.2	54.0	66.8	68.1	72.3

Figure 5.16: Number of Fast Fourier Transform coefficients versus accuracy.

Wavelet

This feature is similar to the other transform based approaches and uses the Wavelet decomposition of the pattern to accomplish its duty. Daubechies wavelet coefficients are used for wavelet transform operation. Overall performance with respect to the size of the feature vector is less than average. Perhaps performance can be improved by utilizing a different type of wavelet instead of Daubechies.

5.4.6   Fractal Based Approaches

The only feature is this subclass is based on the idea of utilizing fractal properties of the pattern.

Fractal Dimension (box counting)

This feature is unique in this experiment as it produces the only 1D feature vector, which holds the fractal dimension of the image calculated using a popular Box Counting approach. This results in the lowest recognition accuracy of all features, but if its size is taken into account, the evaluation drastically changes.

5.4.7   Other Approaches

The features in this subsection don't have much in common, but nonetheless they are very interesting approaches.

Direct Pixel Matching

This approach is unique in a way that it is not a feature extraction methodology at all. Rather, this is just a direct search for the similar pattern as encoded by individual pixels. In order to make the system accept the original pattern as if it was a feature, individual pixels are taken to represent dimensions in the feature vector. The size of this input vector equals to the size of the original image. This situation is the reason for finding different feature extraction methodologies in order to deal with more reasonable amounts of data.

N-tuple

This feature takes measurements at a number of sample points around and within the pattern and records the relationship between them. The most challenging part is the selection of optimal (or just good) sampling locations.

Figure 5.17 shows how with the increasing number of such points performance of this feature also improves. Sampling points in our implementation were selected by visual inspection of patterns, perhaps, systematic determination of sampling locations would produce better performance per unit of information.

Number of N-tuples	1	3	5	10	15	20
Accuracy (%)	19.6	32.7	37.1	44.7	54.9	60.2

Figure 5.17: Number of N-Tuples versus accuracy.

Randomly Generated Feature (for testing)

This was just a control variable in the experiments used to check the correctness of implementation and as the comparison accuracy level for all other features. A random number generator was utilized to produce an array consisting of 25 elements. Not surprisingly performance of this 'feature' resulted in the accuracy consistent with statistically predictable random guessing.

Chapter 6

Conclusions

Now this is not the end. It is not even the beginning of the end.
But it is, perhaps, the end of the beginning.

Sir Winston Churchill (1874 - 1965)

6.1 Accomplishments

Feature extraction methods are as diverse as the people who invent them. As long as we have no shortage of computer scientists, new and improved pattern description methodologies will be proposed. Collecting and organizing such ideas is an important and interesting pursuit.

This book attempted to do just that. The largest known compilation of feature extraction methods for character recognition together with descriptions and evaluations was assembled and classified. A novel feature was included called Fuzzy Zoning, which showed one of the best performance levels of all the tested features. Many different features of various types were implemented and compared in a novel manner, namely utilizing the Normalized Accuracy Measure. As a byproduct of the experiments MLPN and RBFN were optimized and compared, as a result RBFN was judged to be a superior pattern recognizer for the character recognition applications.

The following is a list of the main accomplishments and contributions of this book:

191

1. Large scale review of the *Feature Extraction* (FE) approaches for *Character Recognition* (CR) based on both literature review and experimental results was conducted. Both universal (designed for large number of different data sets) and specific (aimed at a particular type of characters) methods are included in this review.

2. Based on review developed an original classification system, which groups FE methods depending on their theoretical approach. The developed classification system aids in comparison and analysis of the FE methods. Classification has been verified by the CR experiments, which confirmed its validity.

3. Representative subset of all the FE methods reviewed has been selected for more detailed analysis and implementation. The subset included at least a few methods from each cluster generated by the developed classification system.

4. Over thirty programs have been implemented to support the experiments, including neural network classifiers, feature extractors, and experiments controlling software. Experiments were performed using Matlab's Neural Network Toolbox version 3.0 and ran on Intel Celeron processor with clock speed of 1.8 GHz.

5. Analysis, optimization and comparison of two different classifiers, namely MLPN and RBFN were conducted. Neural network's optimal parameters for learning rate, spread, momentum, number of layers, number of nodes and number of epochs for this particular application were found. RBFN was chosen as the superior classifier, both in terms of its speed and accuracy.

6. A novel FE method, called *Fuzzy Zoning* (FZ), was developed. FZ's main competition was with other zoning approaches and unlike all of them, it was designed to counteract the problem of sharp between zone borders. In order to accomplish that, FZ allows a single pixel to contribute to multiple zones at the same time. FZ was analyzed and included in the classification with other zoning based features.

7. Based on experiments and test results, all FE methods were ordered against their respective accuracy in percentages. As this ordering didn't

consider time complexity required for the classifier to work with a particular feature, the size of the feature vectors was taken into consideration for comparison purposes. A new metric was developed, which was called *Normalized Accuracy Measure* (NAM). Unlike a simple accuracy, this metric considers time complexity of feature classification. This approach allows optimizing the total CR operation, which includes both feature extraction and classification.

8. All feature extraction methods were compared and ordered against the developed NAM metric.

Chapter 7

Appendix A: Taxonomy of Geometric Features

1. General

2. 3D from

    (a) 2D Projections

    (b) Line Drawings

3. Boundary/Line/Curve Segmentation

    (a) Breakpoint/Corner Detection

    (b) Lowe's Method

    (c) Multi-Scale Methods

    (d) Recursive Splitting

4. Connected Component Labeling

5. Corner and Interest Point Feature Detectors

    (a) Curvature Scale Space

    (b) Forstner Operator

    (c) Moravec Operator

    (d) Harris/Plessy Corner Finder

    (e) Subpixel Corner Finding

(s) Range/Depth Image Edge Detectors

(t) Regularization Based Edge Detectors

(u) Roberts Cross Edge Detector

(v) Robinson Edge Detector

(w) Second Derivative Operators (including Zero Crossing)

(x) Subpixel Methods (See Subpixel Methods)

(y) Walsh Function/O'Gorman Edge Detector

8. Edge/Line/Contour Feature Following, Grouping, Linking and Tracking

(a) 4/6/8 Connectivity

(b) Contour Tracking

(c) Dynamic Programming

(d) Edge Linking

(e) Graph Searching

(f) Hough Transform (See Transforms: Hough)

(g) Hysteresis Tracking

(h) Paired Boundaries, Paired Contours

(i) Relaxation Linking

(j) Search Trees

(k) Subjective Contours / Illusory Contours

    i. Stochastic Completion Fields

9. Gabor Filters

10. Global Structure Extraction

(a) Ribbons

(b) Salient Features

(c) Symmetry Lines (See also Symmetry)

(d) Symmetry Planes

(f) Line Drawings (See Line Drawings)

(g) Monocular Depth Cues

(h) Monocular Visual Space

(i) Motion

(j) Multiple Sensors (See Multi-Sensor Geometries)

(k) Perspective

(l) Photo-Consistency

(m) Photometric Stereo

(n) Polarization

(o) Shading

(p) Shadows

(q) Specularities

(r) Structured Light

(s) Texture

(t) Texture Motion

(u) Zoom

30. Texture

(a) Boundary Detection

(b) Classification

(c) Color Texture

(d) Filter-based Descriptors

(e) Fourier Descriptors

(f) Hierarchical Textures

(g) Shape Texture/Surface Roughness Characterization

    i. Spectral Scale

31. Structural Texture Representations

(a) Grammatical Representations

32. Statistical Representations

    (a) Co-occurrence, Cocurrence, Cooccurrence Matrices
        i. Color Co-occurrence Matrices
    (b) Edge Frequency
    (c) Energy Measures
    (d) Fractal Measures
    (e) Histogram Methods
    (f) Markov Random Field Representations
    (g) Moments of Intensity (See 2D Moments and their Invariants)
    (h) Primitive Length, Run Length
    (i) Spatial Frequency

33. Texon/Texel Invariants and Representations

34. Texture Field Grouping/Segmentation (See Texture-based Region Segmentation)

35. Texture Gradients/Directions/Oriented Patterns

36. Wavelet Descriptors

37. Topological Image Description

38. Visual Routines, Empirical Feature Detectors

39. Volume Detection

    (a) Voxel Model Recovery
    (b) Generalized Cylinder Estimation
    (c) Superquadric Estimation [48]

Bibliography

[1] Albanesi M. G., Luca Lombardi. Wavelets for Shape Recognition in Image Retrieval: a case study. *Proc. of Workshop on Image and Video Content-Based Retrieval*, pp.81 - 88, 1998.

[2] Amin A., S. Singh, Machine recognition of hand-printed Chinese characters, *Intelligent Data Analysis-An International Journal*, Vol. 1, No. 2, 1998.

[3] Anderson P. G., Roger S. Gaborski. The Polynomial Method Augmented by Supervised Training for Hand-Printed Character Recognition. *International Conference on Artificial Neural Networks and Genetic Algorithms*. Innsbruck, Austria, April 1993.

[4] Anderson P. G., Roger S. Gaborski, David G. Tilley and Christopher T. Asbury. Genetic Algorithm Selection of Features for Handwritten Character Identification. *International Conference on Artificial Neural Networks and Genetic Algorithms*. Innsbruck, Austria, April 1993.

[5] Ashwin T. V., P. S. Sastry. A font and size-independent OCR system for printed Kannada documents using support vector machines. *Sadhana*, Vol. 27, No. 1, pp. 35-58, India, February 2002.

[6] Bailey R. R., Mandyam Srinath. Orthogonal moment features for use with parametric and non-parametric classifiers. *IEEE Transactions on Pattern Analysis and Machine Intelligence*, Vol. 18, No. 4, pp. 389-399, April 1996.

[7] Bajaj R., Lipika Dey and Santanu Chaudhury. Devnagari numeral recognition by combining decision of multiple connectionist classifiers. *dadhana*, Vol. 27, Part 1, pp. 59-72. February 2002.

[8] Baldoni M., Cristina Baroglio, Davide Cavagnino, Giuseppe Lo Bello. *Extraction of discriminant features from image fractal encoding.* Available at: http://www.di.unito.it/ baldoni/fractals, Retrieved March 10, 2003.

[9] Behnke S., Marcus Pfister, and Raul Rojas. Recognition of Handwritten Digits Using Structural Information. (unpublished). Available at: http://www.inf.fu-berlin.de/ rojas/icnn97.ps, Retrieved March 31, 2003.

[10] Belongie s., Jitendra Malik, and Jan Puzicha. Shape matching and object recognition using shape contexts. *IEEE Transactions On Pattern Analysis and Machine Intelligence*, Vol. 24, No. 24, April 2002.

[11] Bianchini M., and M. Gori, Learning without local minima in radial basis function networks. *IEEE Transactions on Neural Networks*, Vol. 6, No. 3, pp.749-756, 1995.

[12] Bledsoe W. W., I. Browning. Pattern recognition and reading by machine. *In 1959 Proceedings of the Eastern Joint Computer Conference*, Vol. 16, pp. 225-232, Dec. 1959.

[13] Blue J. L., G.T.Candela, P.J. Grother, R. Chellappa and C.L. Wilson, Evaluation of Pattern Classifiers for Fingerprint and OCR Applications. *Pattern Recognition*, Vol. 27, No 4, pp. 485-501, April 1994

[14] Boucher A., *An introduction to Fourier series.* Available at: www.rpi.edu/ boucha/fourier.pdf, Retrieved March 10, 2003.

[15] Bourbakis N. G., Gumahad, A.T. Knowledge based text character recognition using Fourier transform. *Proceedings of the 2nd International IEEE Conference on Tools for Artificial Intelligence*, pp. 571-576, 6-9 Nov. 1990

[16] Brandt S., Jorma Laaksonen. Statistical shape features in content-based image retrieval. *Proceedings of ICPR2000*, Barcelona, Spain, September 2000. Available at: http://www.cis.hut.fi/picsom/publications.html, Retrieved March 10, 2003.

[17] Brandt S., *Use of shape features in content-based image retrieval.* Master's thesis. Helsinki University of Technology. August 1999.

[18] Bui T. D., G. Y. Chen and L. Feng. An orthonormal-shell-fourier descriptor for rapid matching of patterns in image database. *International Journal of Pattern Recognition and Artificial Intelligence*, Vol. 15, No. 8, pp. 1213-1229, 2001.

[19] Bui T. D., Guangyi Chen. *Multiresolution Orthonormal Shell-Fourier Descriptor for Pattern Recognition.* Available at: citeseer.nj.nec.com/110875.html, retrieved May 16, 2003.

[20] Burr D. J., Experiments on neural net recognition of spoken and written text. *IEEE transactions on acoustics, speech, and signal processing*, Vol. 36, No. 7, July 1998.

[21] Campilho A., Mohamed Kamel, S. Belkasim. *Image Description using moments.* Available at: http://watfor.uwaterloo.ca/mkamel/SD776/NOTES/note1.pdf, Retrieved March 1, 2003.

[22] Campilho A., Mohamed Kamel, S. Belkasim. *Moment invariants.* Available at: http://watfor.uwaterloo.ca/mkamel/SD776/NOTES/note2.pdf, Retrieved March 1, 2003.

[23] Cao J., M. Ahmadi, and M. Shridhar. Handwritten numeral recognition with multiple features and multistage classifiers. *IEEE Internetional Symposium on Circuits and Systems*, vol. 6, London, pp. 323-326, 1994.

[24] Chan K., A simple yet robust structural approach for recognizing on-line handwritten alphanumerical characters *In Proceedings of the sixth international workshop on frontiers in handwriting recognition*, pp. 229238., 1998.

[25] Chan K., D. Yeung. Recognizing on-line handwritten alphanumeric characters through flexible structural matching. *Pattern Recognition*, Vol. 32, pp. 1099–1114, 1999.

[26] Chen G., Tien D. Bui. Invariant Fourier-wavelet descriptor for patter recognitio. *Pattern Recognition*, volume 32, pp. 1083-1088, 1999.

[27] Chen G., *Applications of wavelet transforms in pattern recognition and de-noising.* Master's thesis. Concordia University, Canada.

[28] Cheung K. W., D.Y. Yeung, R.T. Chin. Recognition of handwritten digits using deformable models. *Proceedings of the Fifth International Workshop on Frontiers in Handwriting Recognition,* pp.259-262, Colchester, England, 2-5 September 1996.

[29] Cheung Y. S., Leung, C.H. Chain-code transform for Chinese character recognition. *Proceedings of IEEE International Conference on Systems, Man, and Cybernetics,* Tucson, Arizona, 1985, pp 42-45.

[30] Chiang A., Liao, S.; Lu, Q.; Pawlak, M. Gegenbauer moment-based applications for Chinese character recognition. *Canadian Conference on Electrical and Computer Engineering,* Vol. 2, pp. 908-911, 12-15 May 2002.

[31] Chiu H. P., Din-Chang Tseng. A novel stroke-based feature extraction for handwritten Chinese character recognition. *Pattern Recognition,* vol. 32, pp. 1947-1959, 1999.

[32] Teh C. H., Roland T. Chin. On image analysis by the methods of moments. *IEEE Transactions on Pattern Analysis and Machine Intelligence,* Vol. PAMI-10, pp. 496-513, July 1988.

[33] Chung Y. Y., M.T.Wong, Handwritten Character Recognition by Fourier Descriptors and Neural Network, *Proc of IEEE International Region 10 Annual Conference - Speech and Image Technologies for Computing and Telecommunications,* pp. 401-404, Brisbane Australia, 2-4 Dec 97.

[34] Suzete E. N., Correia,Joao M. DE Carvalho,Robert Sabourin. *Human-Perception Handwritten Character Recognition using Wavelets,* Available at: citeseer.nj.nec.com/539423.html, retrieved May 3, 2003.

[35] Suzete E. N., Correia, Joo M. de Carvalho, Robert Sabourin. On the Performance of Wavelets for Handwritten Numerals Recognition. *16 th International Conference on Pattern Recognition,* Vol. 3, pp. 30127. Quebec City, QC, Canada. August 11 - 15, 2002.

[36] Dehghan M., Karim Faez. Farsi handwritten character recognition with moment invariants. *Proceedings of 13th International Conference on Digital Signal Processing*, Vol. 2, pp. 507-510, 2-4 July 1997.

[37] Deng D., Chan, K.P., Yinglin Yu. Handwritten Chinese character recognition using spatial Gabor filters and self-organizing feature maps, *Proceedings of IEEE International Conference On Image Processing*, Vol. 3, pp. 940-944, 13-16 Nov. 1994.

[38] Desai R., H.D. Cheng. Pattern Recognition by Local Radial Moments. *Proceedings of the 12th International Conference on Pattern Recognition*, 2, pp. 168-171. Jerusalem, Israel, 1994.

[39] Dimauro G., Gerardi, G.; Impedovo, S.; Pirlo, G.; Tegolo, D. Integration of a structural features-based preclassifier and a man-machine interactive classifier for a fast multi-stroke character recognition. *Proceedings of 11th IAPR International Conference on Pattern Recognition, Conference D: Architectures for Vision and Pattern Recognition*, Vol. 4, pp. 190-194, 30 Aug.-3 Sept. 1992.

[40] Djematene A., B. Taconet, A. Zahour,A geometrical method for printed and handwritten Berber character recognition. *Proceedings of the Fourth International Conference on Document Analysis and Recognition*, Vol. 2, 18-20 Aug. 1997.

[41] Dong Q., *MLP and RBF comparision in a classification problem of a satellite image.* Available at: http://www.stanford.edu/ qfdong/-Work/NN.pdf, Retrieved on April 21, 2003.

[42] Eikvil L., Aas, K., Holden, M. Tools for Automatic Recognition of Character Strings in Maps. *CAIP '95, 6th International Conference on computer analysis of images and patterns* , Prague, Czech Republic, 1995.

[43] El-Desouky A., Salem, M., and Arafat, H. A Handwritten Arabic Character Recognition Technique for Machine Reader. *Int. Journal for Mini Microcomputer*, Vol. 14, No. 2, pp. 57-61, 1992.

[44] Elnagar A., F. Al-Kharousi,S. Harous, Recognition of handwritten Hindi numerals using structural descriptors. *IEEE International Con-*

ference on Systems, Man, and Cybernetics, Vol. 2, pp. 983-988, 12-15 Oct. 1997.

[45] Fan J., *Off-line Optical Character Recognition for Printed Chinese Character-A Surve*. Available at: http://www.ee. columbia.edu/ junfan/E6880Final5.pdf, Retrieved March 10, 2003.

[46] Fan K. C., Wei-Hsien Wu. A run-length coding based approach to stroke extraction of Chinese characters. *Proceedings of 15th International Conference on Pattern Recognition*, pp. 565-568, Vol. 2, 2000.

[47] Finan R. A., A.T. Sapeluk, and R.I. Damper, Comparison of multilayer and radial basis function neural networks for text-dependent speaker recognition. *In Proceedings International Conference on Neural Networks 4*, pp 1992-1997.

[48] Fisher R. B., Geometric Feature Extraction Methods. *CVonline: The Evolving, Distributed, Non-Proprietary, On-Line Compendium of Computer Vision*, Available at: http://homepages.inf.ed.ac.uk/rbf/CVonline/, Retrieved March 5, 2004.

[49] Flusser J., Tomas Suk. Affine moment invariants: A new tool for character recognition. *Pattern Recognition Letters*, Vol. 15, pp. 433-436, 1994.

[50] Flusser J., Tomas Suk. Degraded image analysis: An invariant approach. *pami*, Vol. 20, No. 6, pp. 590–603, June 1998.

[51] Flusser J., Tomas Suk and Stanislav Saic. Recognition of images degraded by linear motion blur without restoration. *Computing, suppl.* 11, pp. 37-51, 1996.

[52] Frohlich J., Types of neural nets. Available at: http://rfhs8012.fh-regensburg.de/ saj39122/jfroehl/diplom/, retrieved April 21, 2003.

[53] Fu K. S., Y. T. Chien, Gerald P. Cardillo. A dynamic programming approach to sequential pattern recognition. *IEEE transactions on pattern analysis and machine intelligence*, Vol. PAMI 8, No. 3, May 1986.

[54] Gan K. W., K.T. Lua, A new approach to stroke and feature point extraction in Chinese character recognition. *Pattern Recognition Letters*, Vol. 12, No. 6, pp. 381-388, 1991.

[55] Garris M. D., R.A. Wilkinson, C.L. Wilson, Analysis of a Biologically Motivated Neural Network for Character Recognition. *Proceedings: Analysis of Neural Network Applications*, ACM Press, George Mason University, May 1991.

[56] Ge Y., Qiang Huo, Zhi-Dan Feng. Offline recognition of handwritten Chinese characters using Gabor features, CDHMM modeling and MCE training. *Proceedings of the IEEE International Conference on Acoustics, Speech, and Signal Processing*, Vol. 1, pp. 1053-1056, 13-17 May 2002.

[57] Glucksman H. A., Classification of mixed-font alphabetics by characteristic loci. *Digest of 1st Ann. IEEE Computer Conference*, pp. 138-141, Chicago, September 1967.

[58] Graps A., An introduction to Wavelets. *IEEE Computational Science and Engineering*, Vol. 2, No. 2, Summer 1995.

[59] Grother P. J., Karhunen Love Feature Extraction for Neural Handwritten Character Recognition. *In Proceedings: Applications of Artificial Neural Networks III*, Orlando, Florida. April 1992.

[60] Hamamoto Y., S. Uchimura, M. Watanabe, T. Yasuda and S. Tomita. Recognition of handwritten numerals using Gabor features. *Proc. of 13th Int. Conf. Pattern Recognition*, Vienna, pp. 250-253, Aug. 1996.

[61] Hamamoto Y., S. Uchimura, K. Masamizu and S. Tomita. Recognition of handprinted Chinese characters using Gabor features. *Proc. of the third Int. Conf. Document Analysis and Recognition*, pp. 819-823, Montreal, Aug. 1995.

[62] Hanmandlu M., Murali Mohan, K.R., Chakraborty, S., Goyal, S. and Choudhury, D.R. Unconstrained handwritten character recognition based on fuzzy logic. *Pattern Recognition*, vol. 36, No. 3, pp. 603-623, August 2003.

[63] Hastie   T.,   R.   Tibshirani.   Handwritten   digit   recogni-
    tion   via   deformable   prototypes,   1993,   Available   at: cite-
    seer.nj.nec.com/hastie94handwritten.html,   retrieved   February   15,
    2004.

[64] Hew P. C., *Moments with respect to Orthogonal Functions*
    on the Unit Disk having Invariance in Form. Diary, Depart-
    ment of Mathematics, The University of Western Australia,
    http://maths.uwa.edu.au/ phew/postgrad/diaries/, March 1998.
    http://citeseer.nj.nec.com/hew96geometric.html, Retrieved March 10,
    2003.

[65] Hew P. C., *Recognition of Printed Digits using Zernike or*
    Orthogonal Fourier-Mellon Moments – 2. Diary, Depart-
    ment of Mathematics, The University of Western Australia,
    http://maths.uwa.edu.au/ phew/postgrad/diaries/, October 1997.
    http://citeseer.nj.nec.com/hew96geometric.html, Retrieved March 10,
    2003.

[66] Hew   P.   C.,   *Reconstruction   from   Zernike   and   Orthog-*
    onal   Fourier-Mellon   Moments.   Diary,   Department   of
    Mathematics,   The   University   of   Western   Australia,
    http://maths.uwa.edu.au/ phew/postgrad/diaries/, February 1997.
    http://citeseer.nj.nec.com/hew96geometric.html, Retrieved March 10,
    2003.

[67] Hew P. C., *Digit Images in Orthogonal Fourier-Mellon Mo-*
    ment Space Diary, Department of Mathematics, The University
    of Western Australia, http://maths.uwa.edu.au/ phew/postgrad/di-
    aries/, March 1997. http://citeseer.nj.nec.com/hew96geometric.html,
    Retrieved March 10, 2003.

[68] Hew P. C., *Zernike or Orthogonal Fourier-Mellon Moments*
    for Representing and Recognizing Printed Digits. Diary, De-
    partment of Mathematics, The University of Western Aus-
    tralia,   http://maths.uwa.edu.au/   phew/postgrad/diaries/,
    http://citeseer.nj.nec.com/hew96geometric.html,   Retrieved   March
    10, 2003.

[69] Hong W., *Comparison of Basic Techniques and Tangent Distance for Handwritten Digit Recognition*, Networks, Approximation, and Learning - 9.520, MIT, Spring 1996. Available at: http://www.ai.mit.edu/people/jesse/www/papers/ Retrieved, May 22, 2003.

[70] Hu P., Yannan Zhao, Zehong Yang, Jiaqin Wang. Recognition of gray character using gabor filters. *Proceedings of the Fifth International Conference on Information Fusion*, Vol. 1, pp. 419-424, 8-11 July 2002.

[71] Hu J., Hong Yan, Structural decomposition and description of printed and handwritten characters. *Proceedings of the 13th International Conference on Pattern Recognition*, Vol. 3, pp. 230-234, 25-29 Aug. 1996.

[72] Huang L., Xiao Huang. Multiresolution recognition of offline handwritten Chinese characters with wavelet transform. *Proceedings of the Sixth International Conference on Document Analysis and Recognition*, pp. 631-634, 10-13 Sept. 2001.

[73] Huo Q., Ge Y., Feng Z. High Performance Chinese OCR Based on Gabor Features, Discriminative Feature Extraction and Model Training. *2001 IEEE International Conference on Acoustics, Speech, and Signal Processing*, 4pp, Salt Lake City, USA, 2001.

[74] Huo Q., Feng Z., Ge Y., A Study on the Use of Gabor Features for Chinese OCR. *2001 International Symposium on Intelligent Multimedia, Video and Speech Processing (ISIMP-2001)*. Hong Kong, 2001, 389-392.

[75] Hussain S., G. T. Toussaint, and R. W. Donaldson. Results obtained using a simple character recognition procedure on Munson's handprinted data. *IEEE Trans. On Computers,* pp. 201-205, February 1972.

[76] Iftekharuddin K. M., T. Schechinger, K. Jemili, M.A. Karim. A feature-based neural wavelet optical character recognition, *Optical Engineering*, Vol. 34, pp. 3193-3199, 1995.

[77] Iivarinen J., A. Visa. Shape recognition of irregular objects. In D. P. Casasent, editor, *Intelligent Robots and Computer Vision XV: Algorithms, Techniques, Active Vision, and Materials Handling*, Proc. SPIE 2904, pp. 25-32, 1996.

[78] Jain A. K., Douglas E. Zongker. Representation and Recognition of Handwritten Digits Using Deformable Templates. *IEEE Transactions on Pattern Analysis and Machine Intelligence 19*, Vol. 12, pp.1386-1391, 1997.

[79] Jennings C., *Character recognition using the Hough transform*. Technical Report 93/51/22, University of Calgary, March 1993.

[80] Jeong C. S., Dong-Seok Jeong. Hand-written digit recognition using Fourier descriptors and contour information. *Proceedings of the IEEE Region 10 Conference TENCON 99*, Vol. 2 , pp. 1283-1286, 15-17 Sept. 1999.

[81] Jin L. W., K.P. Chan, B.Z. Xu, A Deformable Elastic Matching Model for Handwritten Chinese Character Writing, *Proc. 1995 IEEE Int. Conf. on Systems, Man and Cybernetics*, Vol. 3, pp. 1945-1950, Vancouver, Canada, Oct., 1995.

[82] Jun Y., Yu Songyu; Zhao Rongchun. Wavelet analysis for handwritten Chinese character recognition. *IEEE International Conference on Intelligent Processing Systems* , Vol. 2, pp. 1023-1026, 28-31 Oct. 1997

[83] Jung M. C., Yong-Chul Shin; Srihari, S.N. Machine printed character segmentation method using side profiles. *1999 IEEE International Conference on Systems, Man, and Cybernetics*, Vol. 6, pp. 863-867, 1999.

[84] Jung D. M., M. S. Krishnamoorthy, George Nagy, and Andrew Shapira. N-tuple features for OCR revisited. *IEEE Transactions on Pattern Analysis and Machine Intelligence,* Vol. 18, No. 7, July 1996.

[85] Kapoor R., D. Begai, T. Kamal, Representation and extraction of nodal features of DevNagri letters. *Indian Conference on Computer Vision, Graphics and Image processing*, December 16-18, 2002.

[86] Khofanzad A., Chung, C. Handwritten digit recognition using combination of neural network classifiers. *Image Analysis and Interpretation, 1998 IEEE Southwest Symposium on*, pp. 168-173, 5-7 Apr 1998.

[87] Khotanzad A., Yaw Hua Hong. Rotation invariant pattern recognition using Zernike moments. *9th International Conference on Pattern Recognition*, Vol. 1, pp. 326-328, 14-17 Nov. 1988.

[88] Khotanzad A., Yaw Hua Hong. Invariant image recognition by Zernike moments. *IEEE Transactions on Pattern Analysis and Machine Intelligence*, pp. 489-497, Vol. 12, No. 5, May 1990.

[89] Kimura F., M. Shridhar. Handwritten numerical recognition based on multiple algorithms. *Pattern Recognition*, Vol. 24, No. 10, pp. 969-983, 1991.

[90] Krzyzak A., Leung, S.Y.; Suen, C.Y. Reconstruction of two dimensional patterns by Fourier descriptors. *9th International Conference on Pattern Recognition*, pp. 555-558, vol.1, 14-17 Nov. 1988.

[91] Kushnir M., Keiichi Ave, and Kinji Matsumoto. Recognition of handprinted Hebrew characters using features selected in the hough transform space. *Pattern Recognition*, Vol. 18, No. 2, pp. 103-114, 1985.

[92] Kyrki V., Kamarainen, J.-K., Kalviainen, H., Invariant Shape Recognition Using Global Gabor Features. *In Proceedings of the 12th Scandinavian Conference on Image Analysis*, pp. 671-678, Bergen, Norway, 2001.

[93] Kim S. H., J.I. Doh. Off-line Recognition of Korean Scripts using Distance Matching and Neural Network Classifiers, *Proc. 3rd International Conference on Document Analysis and Recognition*, pp. 34-37, Montreal, Canada, Aug. 1995.

[94] Laaksonen J., Subspace Classifiers in Recognition of Handwritten Digits. Doctoral thesis. Acta Polytechnica Scandinavica Ma 84, Espoo, April 1997.

[95] Laine A. F., Sergio Schuler. *Hexagonal wavelet representations for recognizing complex annotations.* Available at: http://medimage.bme.columbia.edu/publication.dir/papers.dir/, Retrieved May 2, 2003.

[96] Dimauro G., S. Impedovo, G. Pirlo and A. Salzo. Zoning Design for Handwritten Numeral Recognition. *ICIAP*, vol. 2, pp.592-599, 1997.

[97] Lee L. L., M. G. L. Espinosa, N. R. Gomes e A. Koerich, "A Prototype for Brazilian Bankcheck Recognition", International Journal of Pattern Recognition and Artificial Intelligence - IJPRAI, Vol. 11. No. 4, pp. 549-569, 1997.

[98] Lee S. J., H.L. Tsai, Pattern fusion in feature recognition neural networks for handwritten character recognition. *IEEE transactions on systems, man, and cybernetics - part B: Cybernetics,* Vol. 28, No. 4, August 1998.

[99] Leung C. H., L. Sze. Feature selection in the recognition of handwritten Chinese characters. *Engineering Applications of Artificial Intelligence,* vol. 10, No 5, pp. 495-502, 1997.

[100] Li X., Dit Yan Yeung. On-line handwritten alphanumeric character recognition using dominant points in strokes. *Pattern Recognition,* Vol. 30, No. 1, pp. 31-44, January 1997.

[101] Liao S., Q. Lu. A Study of Moment Functions and Its Use in Chinese Character Recognition, *Fourth International Conference on Document Analysis and Recognition,* pp. 572-575, Ulm, Germany, August 18-20, 1997.

[102] Liao S., Amy Chiang, Qin Lu, and Miroslaw Pawlak. Chinese Character Recognition via Gegenbauer Moments. *The 16th International Conference on Pattern Recognition,* Aug. 11 - 15, 2002, Quebec City, Canada.

[103] Liao S. X., Miroslaw Pawlak. On image analysis by moments. *IEEE Transactions on Pattern Analysis and Machine Intelligence,* Vol. 18, No. 3, pp. 254-266, March 1996.

[104] Liao S., Miroslaw Pawlak. Image analysis with moment descriptor. *The Proceedings of 7th International Conference on Signal Processing Applications & Technology,* Vol. 1, pp. 987-991, Boston, October 7-10, 1996.

[105] Lim J.H., Teh, H.H. Lui, H.C. Wang, P.Z. Fitting elastic maps to recognize handwritten digits. *Proceedings of the IEEE International Conference on Neural Networks,* Vol. 6, pp. 3078-3082, 27 Nov.-1 Dec. 1995.

[106] Lin F., Xiaoou Tang. Off-line handwritten Chinese character stroke extraction. *in Proc. of International Conf. on Pattern Recognition*, Vancouver, Canada, Aug. 2002.

[107] Liu C. L., In-Jung Kim, Jin H. Kim. Model-based stroke extraction and matching for handwritten Chinese character recognition. *Pattern Recognition*, vol. 34, pp. 2339-2352, 2001.

[108] Liu K., Y.S. Huang, and C.Y. Suen, Identification of Fork Points on the Skeletons of Handwritten Chinese Characters, *IEEE Transactions on Pattern Analysis and Machine Intelligence*, Vol. 21, No. 10, pp. 1095-1100, 1999.

[109] Liu K., Y.S. Huang, and C.Y. Suen, Robust stroke segmentation method for handwritten Chinese character recognition. *Proceedings of the Fourth International Conference on Document Analysis and Recognition*, Vol. 1, pp. 211-215, 18-20 Aug. 1997.

[110] Gang L., Wu Di, Guo Jun, Hong Gang Zhang, A New Feature Extraction Method Based on Fourier Transform in Handwriting Digits Recognition, *Proc. of 2002 International Conference on Machine Learning and Cybernetics*, Nov. 2002.

[111] Loncaric S., A survey of shape analysis techniques. *Pattern Recognition*, Vol. 31, No. 8, pp. 983-1001, 1998.

[112] Lu Q., K. H. Lee. Recognition of Chinese Characters by Moment Feature Extraction. *17th International Conference on Computer Processing of Oriental Languages*, pp. 566-571, Hong Kong, April 2-4, 1997.

[113] Lu Z., Z. Chi, W.-C. Siuand P.-F. Shi. A New Templates Presentation and Extraction Method for Handwritten Digit Recognition. *Asian Technology Information Program*, Japan, 1998.

[114] Lucas S., Amiri, A. Recognition of chain-coded handwritten character images with scanning n-tuple method. *Electronics Letters*, Vol. 31, No. 24, pp. 2088-2089, 23 Nov 1995.

[115] Lursinsap C., Khunasaraphan, C. Simulated light sensitive model for handwritten digit recognition. *International Joint Conference on Neural Networks, IJCNN*, Vol. 4, pp. 13-18, 7-11 Jun 1992.

[116] Maddouri S., H.Amiri and A. Belad, Local Normalization Towards Global Recognition of Arabic Handwritten Script, *Document Analysis and Systems (DAS'00)*, December 2000, Rio, Brasil.

[117] Man G. M. T., Poon, J.C.H. An enhanced approach to character recognition by Fourier descriptor. *Communications on the Move Singapore ICCS/ISITA*, pp. 558-562 vol.2, 16-20 Nov. 1992.

[118] Matsuura T., Tangtisanon, P.; Thumwarin, P. *The 2000 IEEE Asia-Pacific Conference on On-line Thai numeral recognition Circuits and Systems*, pp. 445-448, 4-6 Dec. 2000.

[119] Maurycy S., *A comparative study of statistically classifiable features used within the area of Optical Character Recognition.* Master Thesis, Image Processing Laboratory, University of Oslo, Norway, 1995.

[120] McGregor D., *Model-based neural networks for invariant pattern recognition.* Ph. D. Thesis. Curtin University of Technology. October 1996.

[121] Methasate I., Sutat Sae-Tang. On-line Thai Handwriting Character Recognition Using Stroke Segmentation With HMM. *Applied Informatics International Symposium on Artificial Intelligence and Applications*, Innsbruck, Austria, pp 59-62, 18-21 Feb 2002.

[122] Mezghani N., Mitiche, A.; Cheriet, M. On-line recognition of handwritten Arabic characters using a Kohonen neural network. *Proceedings of the Eighth International Workshop on Frontiers in Handwriting Recognition* , pp. 490 -495, 6-8 Aug. 2002.

[123] Ming C. Y., *Shape-based image retrieval in iconic image databases.* Master's thesis. Chinese University of Hong Hong. June 1999.

[124] Mizukami Y., A handwritten Chinese character recognition system using hierarchical displacement extraction based on directional features. *Pattern Recognition Letters*, vol. 19, pp. 595-604, 1998.

[125] Mori M., Minako Sawaki, Norihiro Hagita. Category-Dependent Feature Extraction for Recognition of Degraded Handwritten Characters. *16th International Conference on Pattern Recognition*, vol.3, pp.155-159, Quebec, Canada, Aug. 2002

[126] Mori M., Sawaki, M.; Hagita, N.; Murase, H.; Mukawa, N.Robust feature extraction based on run-length compensation for degraded handwritten character recognition. *Proceedings of Sixth International Conference on Document Analysis and Recognition*, pp. 650-654, 2001.

[127] Mori S., Hirobumi Nishida, Hiromitsu Yamada. *Optical Character Recognition*. Willey Series in Microwave and Optical Engineering. Japan, 1999.

[128] Morns I. P., S.S. Dlay, The DSFPN, a new neural network for optical character recognition. *IEEE transactions on neural networks*, Vol. 10, No. 6. November 1999.

[129] Mowlaei A., Faez, K.; Haghighat, A.T. Feature extraction with wavelet transform for recognition of isolated handwritten Farsi/Arabic characters and numerals. *14th International Conference on Digital Signal Processing*, Vol. 2, pp. 923-926, 1-3 July 2002.

[130] Mukundan R., Ong, S.H.; Lee, P.A. Image analysis by Tchebichef moments. *IEEE Transactions on Image Processing*, Vol. 10, No. 9, pp. 1357-1364, Sept. 2001.

[131] Neumann B., Computer Vision. Available at: emphkogs-www.informatik.uni-hamburg.de/Vorlesungen/material/bvss02/BVVorlesungWoche5.pdf, Retrieved June 10, 2003.

[132] Nishida H., Structural feature extraction using multiple bases. *Computer Vision and Image Understanding*, vol. 62, No. 1, pp. 78-89, 1995.

[133] Oja E., J. Laaksonen, and L. Tuura, Application of Statistical and Neural Classifiers to Recognition of Handwritten Digits. Quinquennial report. Available at: http://www.cis.hut.fi/research/reports/ quinquennial/, retrieved on April 21, 2003.

[134] Okamoto M., Kazuhiko Yamamoto. On-line handwriting character recognition using direction-change features that consider imaginary strokes. *Pattern Recognition* , vol. 32, pp. 1115-1128, 1999.

[135] Ozn O., O.F. Ozer, C.O. Tuzel, V. Atalay, A.E. Cetin. Vision-based Single-stroke Character Recognition for Wearable Computing. *IEEE Intelligent Systems*, Vol.16, pp.33-37, 2001.

[136] Park J., V. Govindaraju, Active Character Recognition Using A*-like Algorithm, *IEEE Conference on Computer Vision and Pattern Recognition*, Hilton Head Island, South Carolina, 2000.

[137] Park J. W., R.G. Harley, and G.K. Venayagamoorthy, Comparison of MLP and RBF Neural Networks Using Deviation Signals for On-Line Identification of a Synchronous Generator. *in Proc. of IEEE PES Winter Meeting*, New York, Vol.1, pp. 274-279, January 2002.

[138] Parker J. R., Bateman, L., Baumback, M., Scale Effects in Shadow Masks for Signature Verification. *2002 International Conference on Artificial Intelligence, (IC-AI'02)*, Las Vegas, USA, June 24-27, 2002.

[139] Parker J. R., *Vector templates for hand-printed symbol recognition.* Available at: pharos.cpsc.ucalgary.ca/Dienst/Repository/2.0/Body/ncstrl. ucalgarycs/1995-559-11/, Retrieved May 2, 2003.

[140] Parker J. R., *Stroke extraction for handprinted digit recognition.* Available at: pharos.cpsc.ucalgary.ca/Dienst/Repository/2.0/Body/ncstrl. ucalgarycs/1995-559-11/, Retrieved May 2, 2003.

[141] Pawlak M., Simon X. Liao. On image analysis by orthogonal moments. *Proceedings of 11th IAPR International Conference on Pattern Recognition, Conference C: Image, Speech and Signal Analysis*, Vol. 3, pp. 549-552, 30 Aug.-3 Sept. 1992

[142] Pawlak M., On the reconstruction aspects of moment descriptors. *Information Theory, IEEE Transactions on*, Vol. 38, No. 6, pp. 1698-1708, Nov. 1992.

[143] Pisit P., Kimpan Chom, Sato Makoto. A Rough Ring Projection Method for Invariant Thai Character Recognition. *International Conference on Information Systems, Analysis and Synthesis*, Vol. 7, 2001.

[144] Ping Z., Chen Lihui. A novel feature extraction method and hybrid tree classification for handwritten numerical recognition. *Pattern Recognition Letters*, vol. 23, pp. 45-56, 2002.

[145] Thool R. C., T. R. Sontakke. *Statistical Pattern Recognition technique for character recognition.* Available at: http://semioweb.msh-paris.fr/escom/projetsrecherche/ 0102projetinde/IEMCTRecognition/ThoolRecognition.pdf, Retrived March 10, 2003.

[146] Tsang I. J., I.R. Tsang and D. Van Dyck. Handwritten Character Recognition Based on Moment Features Derived From Image Partition. *Proc. Fifth IEEE Inter. Conf. on Image Processing*, Chicago, IL, 1998.

[147] Ren T. I., *Pattern recognition and complex systems.* Ph. D. Thesis. University of Antwerpen. 2000.

[148] Revow M., C.K.I. Williams, G.E. Hinton, Using Generative Models for Handwritten Digit Recognition, emphIEEE Transactions on Pattern Analysis and Machine Intelligence, Vol. 18, No. 6, pp. 592-606, 1996.

[149] Pinales J. R., Eric Lecolinet. Cursive Handwriting Recognition Using the Hough Transform and a Neural Network. *International Conference on Pattern Recognition*, Vol. 2. Barcelona, Spain. September 03 - 08, 2000.

[150] Sabaei M., Faez, K. Unsupervised classification of handwritten Farsi numerals using evolution strategies. *Proceedings of IEEE Conference on Speech and Image Technologies for Computing and Telecommunications*, Vol. 1, pp. 403-406, 2-4 Dec. 1997.

[151] Sabourin R., Cheriet, M.; Genest, G. An extended-shadow-code based approach for off-line signature verification. *Document Analysis and Recognition, Proceedings of the Second International Conference on*, pp. 1-5, 20-22 Oct 1993.

[152] Sabourin R., Genest, G. An extended-shadow-code based approach for off-line signature verification. I. Evaluation of the bar mask definition. *Proceedings of the 12th IAPR International. Conference on Pattern Recognition - Conference B: Computer Vision & Image Processing*, Vol. 2, pp. 450-453, 9-13 Oct 1994.

[153] Sabourin R., Genest, G. An extended-shadow-code based approach for off-line signature verification. II. Evaluation of several multi-classifier combination strategies. *Document Analysis and Recognition, Proceedings of the Third International Conference on*, Vol. 1, pp. 197-201, 14-16 Aug 1995.

[154] Sarle W. S., *How do MLPs compare with RBFs?* Available at ftp://ftp.sas.com/pub/neural/FAQ2.html. Last-modified: 2002-10-11, retrieved April 19, 2002.

[155] Sasi S., Loren Schwiebert and Jatinder Singh Bedi. Wavelet Packet Transform And Neuro-Fuzzy Approach To Handwritten Character Recognition. Available at: http://citeseer.nj.nec.com/184862.html, Retrieved March 31, 2003.

[156] Scattolin P., Recognition of handwritten numerals using elastic matching. Master's Thesis, Concordia University, Canada 1995, Available at: citeseer.nj.nec.com/scattolin95recognition.html, Retrieved February 15, 2004.

[157] Shen D., Horace H.S. Ip. Discriminative wavelet shape descriptors for recognition of 2-D patterns. *Pattern recognition*, volume 32, pp. 151-165, 1999.

[158] Shioyama T., Hamanaka, J. Recognition algorithm for handprinted Chinese characters by 2D-FFT. *Proceedings of the 13th International Conference on Pattern Recognition*, Vol. 3, pp. 225-229 , 25-29 Aug. 1996.

[159] Shirali-Shahreza M. H., Faez, K.; Khotanzad, A. Recognition of handwritten Persian/Arabic numerals by shadow coding and an edited probabilistic neural network. *Proceedings of International Conference on Image Processing*, Vol. 3, pp. 436-439, 23-26 Oct 1995.

[160] Singh S., M Hewitt. Cursive digit and character recognition on CEDAR database. *Proc.15th International Conference on Pattern Recognition*, Barcelona, IEEE Press 2, pp. 569-572, 2000.

[161] Sinha A., An improved recognition module for the identification of handwritten digits. Master's thesis. Massachusetts Institute of Technology. May 21, 1999.

[162] Smagt P. V. D., A comparative study of neural network algorithms applied to optical character recognition. *Proceedings of the third international conference on Industrial and engineering applications of artificial intelligence and expert systems*, pp. 1037-1044, Charleston, South Carolina, United States, 1990.

[163] Starner T., *Handwritten Digit Recognition.* Available at: http://www.cc.gatech.edu/classes/AY2000/cs7495fall/ participants/-jammin/fp/, retrieved March 23, 2003.

[164] Su Y. M., Wang, J.-F. A novel stroke extraction method for Chinese characters using Gabor filters. *Pattern Recognition*, vol. 36, No. 3, pp. 635-647, September 2001.

[165] Su Y. M., Jhing-Fa Wang, A learning process to the identification of feature points on Chinese characters, *Proceedings of the 16th International Conference on Pattern Recognition*, Vol. 3, pp. 93-97, 11-15 Aug. 2002.

[166] Suh J., J. Kim, *Stroke Extraction from Gray-Scale Character Image*, Available at: http://aim.kaist.ac.kr/ suh/, retrieved February 10, 2004.

[167] Sural S., P.K. Das. An MLP using Hough transform based fuzzy feature extraction for Bengali script recognition. *Pattern Recognition Letters*, vol. 20, pp. 771-782, 1999. http://www.ee.iitb.ac.in/ icvgip/PAPERS/171.pdf, Retrieved March 31, 2003.

[168] Sural S., and P. K. Das. Fuzzy Hough transform and an MLP with fuzzy input/output for character recognition, *Fuzzy Sets and Systems* Vol. 105, pp. 489-497, 1999.

[169] Sural S., P.K. Das. *A Soft Computing Approach to Character Recognition*, available at: citeseer.nj.nec.com/550796.html, retrieved March 10, 2003.

[170] Tang Y. Y., Suen, C.Y. Extraction of peripheral shape features in Chinese character recognition. *Proceedings of the 12th IAPR International Conference on Pattern Recognition, Conference B: Computer Vision & Image Processing*, Vol. 2, pp. 377-379, 9-13 Oct 1994.

[171] Tang Y. Y., Bing F. Li, Hong Ma, and Jiming Liu. Ring-Projection-Wavelet-Fractal Signatures: A novel approach to feature extraction. *IEEE Transactions On Circuits and Systems II: Analog and Digital Signal Processing*, Vol. 45, No. 8. August 1998.

[172] Tang Y. Y., Bing F. Li, Hong Ma, Jiming Liu, C.H.Leung and Ching Y. Suen. A novel approach to optical character recognition based on ring-projection-wavelet-fractal signatures, *ICPR*, Vol. 2, pp. 325-329, 1996.

[173] Tang Y. Y., H. D. Cheng, & C. Y. Suen. Transformation-Ring-Projection (TRP) Algorithm and Its VLSI Implementation, *Character & Handwriting Recognition: Expanding Frontiers*, World Scientific Publishing Co. Pte. Ltd., Singapore, 1991.

[174] Tang Y. Y., Yu Tao, and Ernest C.M. Lam. New method for feature extraction based on fractal behavior. *Pattern Recognition*, Vol. 35, No. 5, pp. 1071-1081, 2002.

[175] Tanomaru J., Inubushi, A. A compact representation of binary patterns for invariant recognition. *Systems, Man and Cybernetics, Intelligent Systems for the 21st Century.*, *IEEE International Conference on*, Vol. 2, pp. 1550 -1555, 22-25 Oct 1995.

[176] Tanomaru J., Inubushi, A. A simple coding scheme for neural recognition of binary visual patterns. *Neural Networks, 1995. Proceedings.*, *IEEE International Conference on*, Vol. 5, pp. 2432 -2437, Nov/Dec 1995.

[177] Tao Y., Thomas Richard Ioerger and Yuan Y. Tang. Extraction of rotation invariant signature based on fractal geometry. Available at: faculty.cs.tamu.edu/ioerger/ICIP-01-Tao.pdf, Retrieved March 10, 2003.

[178] Tao Y., Lam, C.M. and Tang, Y.Y. Extraction of Fractal Feature for Pattern Recognition, *Proc. of the 15th Inter. Conf. on Pattern Recognition* (ICPR 2000), Vol. 2, pp. 527-530, Barcelona, Spain, September 2000.

[179] Tavsanoglu V., and Saatci, E. Feature Extraction for Character Recognition Using Gabor-type Filters Implemented by Cellular Neural Networks. *Proc. 6th IEEE International Workshop on Cellular Neural Networks and Their Applications (CNNA 2000)*, pp. 63-68, Catania, Italy, May 2000.

[180] Taxt T., Bjerde, K.W. Classification of handwritten vector symbols using elliptic Fourier descriptors. *Proceedings of the 12th IAPR International Conference on Pattern Recognition - Conference B: Computer Vision and Image Processing* , Vol. 2, pp. 123 -128, 9-13 Oct. 1994.

[181] Teredesai A., E. Ratzlaf, J. Subrahmonia, V. Govindaraju. On-Line Digit Recognition using Off-Line Features, *Indian Conference on Computer Vision, Graphics and Image Processing*, 2002. Available at: www.ee.iitb.ac.in/ icvgip/PAPERS/321.pdf, Retrieved April 1, 2003.

[182] Tham Y. M., Tong Lee, Four corner code based pre-classification scheme for Chinese character recognition. *International Symposium on Speech, Image Processing and Neural Networks*, Hong Kong, 13-16 April 1994.

[183] Torres-Mendez L. A., J. C. Ruiz-Suarez, Luis E. Sucar and G. Gomez. Translation, rotation, and scale-invariant object recognition. *IEEE transactions on systems, man, and cybernetics- part C: applications and reviews*, Vol. 30, No. 1, February 2000.

[184] Torok L., Tibor Katona, Jozsef Voros, Endre Jofoldi. *Handwritten Numeral Recognition: CARE - Computer Aided Recognition*. Available at: http://web.axelero.hu/jendre/writings/careengl.pdf, Retrieved April 28, 2003.

[185] Trier O. D., Anil K. Jain, and Torfinn Taxt. Feature Extraction Methods For Character Recognition - A Survey. *Pattern Recognition*, Vol. 29, No. 4, pp. 641-662, 1996.

[186] Toraichi K., Tadahiko Kumamoto, Kazuhiko Yamamoto, Hiromitsu Yamada. Feature analysis of handprinted Chinese characters. *Pattern Recognition Letters*, Vol 17, No. 7, pp.795-800, 1996.

[187] Toussaint   G.,   *Moments.*   Available   at:
      http://cgm.cs.mcgill.ca/   godfried/teaching/pr-notes/moments.ps,
      Retrieved June 22, 2003.

[188] Wang A. B., Kuo-Chin Fan. Optical recognition of handwritten Chinese
      characters by hierarchical radical matching method. *Pattern Recogni-*
      tion, vol. 34, pp. 15-35, 2001.

[189] XueWen W., Ding XiaoQing, Liu ChangSong. Optimized Gabor filter
      based feature extraction for character recognition. *Proceedings of the*
      16th international conference on pattern recognition, Vol. 4, pp.223-226,
      2002.

[190] XueWen W., Ding XiaoQing, Liu ChangSong, Optimized Gabor filter
      based feature extraction for character recognition. *Proceedings of the*
      16th international conference on pattern recognition, Vol. 4, pp.223-226,
      2002.

[191] Whichello A. P., Hong Yan. Reconstruction of Character Skeletons
      using Gabor filter features. *Electronics Letters.* Vol. 31, No. 22, pp.
      1911-1912, 26th October 1995.

[192] William A., Off-line cursive handwritten recognition using recurrent
      neural networks. Ph. D. Thesis. University of Cambridge. September
      1994.

[193] Wong W., Wan-chi Siu; Kin-man Lam. Automatic generation of mo-
      ment invariants and the use of higher order moments for character
      recognition. *IEEE International Symposium on Circuits and Systems*,
      pp. 559-562, 3-6 May 1993.

[194] Xue H., and V. Govindaraju, Character Recognition by Matching Se-
      quences of Pseudo-stroke Positions and Directions. *Proceedings Seventh*
      International Workshop on Frontiers of Handwriting Recognition, Am-
      sterdam, The Netherlands, September 2000, pp. 589-594.

[195] Yamada K., Optimal sampling intervals for Gabor features and printed
      Japanese character recognition. *Proceedings of the Third International*
      Conference on Document Analysis and Recognition, Vol. 1, pp. 150-153,
      14-16 Aug. 1995.

[196] Yampolskiy R. V., D.V. Novikov, Experimental Study of the Choice Between MLP and RBF Neural Networks for Character Recognition. *WNYIPW - IEEE Signal Processing Society*, Rochester NY, October 2003.

[197] Yang J., Jing-yu Yang. Generalized K-L transform based combined feature extraction. *Pattern Recognition*, vol. 35, pp. 295-297, 2002.

[198] Yap P. T., Raveendran, P., Ong, S.H. Krawtchouk moments as a new set of discrete orthogonal moments for image reconstruction. *Proceedings of the 2002 International Joint Conference on Neural Networks* Vol. 1, pp. 908-912, 12-17 May 2002.

[199] Yap P. T., Raveendran, P. Image restoration of noisy images using Tchebichef moments. *Asia-Pacific Conference on Circuits and Systems*, pp. 525-528, Vol. 2, 28-31 Oct. 2002.

[200] Yap P. T., Raveendran, P.; Ong, S.H.; Chebyshev moments as a new set of moments for image reconstruction. *Proceedings of International Joint Conference on Neural Networks*, Vol. 4, pp. 2856-2860, 15-19 July 2001.

[201] Yap P. T., Paramesran, R.; Seng-Huat Ong. Image analysis by Krawtchouk moments. *IEEE Transactions on Image Processing*, vol. 12, num 11, pp. 1367-1377, November 2003.

[202] Yoshimura H., Minoru Etoh, Kenji Kondo, Naokazu Yokoya, Gray-Scale Character Recognition by Gabor Jets Projection. *International Conference on Pattern Recognition*, Vol. 2, pp. 2335-2338, 2000.

[203] Yuen H., A chain coding approach for real-time recognition of on-line handwritten characters. *Conference Proceedings of IEEE International Conference on Acoustics, Speech, and Signal Processing*, Vol. 6, pp. 3426-3429, 7-10 May 1996.

[204] Yuen H., Li, C.K. Handwriting and bilevel graphics coding based on quadtree segmented block-run run-length coding. *Proceedings of IEEE TENCON on Digital Signal Processing Applications*, Vol. 2, pp. 712-715, 26-29 Nov 1996.

[205] Zeki A. M., Zakaria, M.S. New primitives to reduce the effect of noise for handwritten features extraction. *Proceedings of TENCON*, Vol. 2, pp. 403-408, 2000.

[206] Zhang S., B. Taconet, A. Faure, A complexity measure based algorithm for multifont Chinese character recognition. *Proceedings of the 10th International Conference on Pattern Recognition*, Vol. i, pp. 573-577, 16-21 June 1990.

[207] Zhang P., Bui, T.D.; Suen, C.Y. Recognition of similar objects using 2-D wavelet-fractal feature extraction. *Proceedings of the 16th International Conference on Pattern Recognition*, Vol. 2, pp. 316-319, 11-15 Aug. 2002.

www.ingramcontent.com/pod-product-compliance
Lightning Source LLC
Chambersburg PA
CBHW021426180326
41458CB00001B/147